AI-POWERED LIBRARIES

A Practical Guide to Transforming Services and Operations

By

Dr. Hesham Mohamed Elsherif

Dr. Salwa Elmeawad

ABOUT THE AUTHOR

Dr. Hesham Mohamed Elsherif stands at the forefront of library management, research, and the practical implementation of Artificial Intelligence (AI) in educational and library systems. With over 22 years of dedicated service in the field, he brings a wealth of expertise that bridges the worlds of technology, organizational leadership, and scholarship.

Dr. Elsherif's academic credentials are as diverse as they are impressive. He holds two doctoral degrees—one in **Management and Organizational Leadership** and the other in **Information Systems and Technology**. This dual specialization has equipped him with a holistic perspective on how institutions can effectively integrate emerging technologies, particularly AI, to optimize resource allocation, streamline operational processes, and enrich learning experiences.

A recognized authority in **empirical research methodology**, Dr. Elsherif specializes in **qualitative approaches** and **action research**. His mastery of these methodologies has not only bolstered his own scholarly work but has also allowed him to pioneer new ways of investigating and implementing AI-driven solutions in school, academic, and public libraries. Whether he is designing user-centric AI tools or conducting in-depth studies on technology adoption, Dr. Elsherif's methodical and data-driven approach consistently yields impactful, real-world results.

Over the years, he has made significant strides in shaping the academic community - not just as a **professional researcher**, but also as an **Adjunct Professor**. In the classroom, Dr. Elsherif has a remarkable ability to translate complex theories into accessible insights, thereby training a new generation of thought leaders and specialists in both library science and technology. This multifaceted role, spanning teaching, research, and practice, has cemented his status as a **pioneer** whose influence extends well beyond traditional academic boundaries.

Dr. Elsherif's expertise and passion are truly global in scope. He has served as a **consultant to numerous educational institutions worldwide**, offering guidance on best practices, AI integration strategies, and effective management models. His international collaborations speak to the versatility of his knowledge, which is informed by a deep understanding of how AI can enhance resource discovery, user engagement, and scholarly communication across cultural and institutional contexts.

Central to Dr. Elsherif's mission is the belief that **innovative technologies**, including AI, must be harnessed responsibly and ethically. This commitment is evident in his approach to library management and educational technology, where he advocates for solutions that are inclusive, data-secure, and aligned with the core values of academic freedom and public service. By focusing on ethical implementation, he ensures that advancements in AI serve learners, educators, and researchers effectively and fairly.

Today, Dr. Elsherif continues to break new ground in **library innovation, academic research**, and **technology leadership**. Combining a passion for education with an unparalleled depth of knowledge, he remains a guiding force - **inspiring, educating, and leading** in library systems, educational institutions, and beyond. Through his work, he illuminates the path toward a future where AI seamlessly complements human expertise, thereby enriching the academic and public spheres for generations to come.

3

Dr. Salwa Elmeawad emerges as a distinguished leader in both the academic and community service arenas, with specialized expertise as an AI specialist applying artificial intelligence in education and library systems. Serving as the Adult Services Manager at Queens Library, she has harnessed AI technologies to transform information access and literacy programs, enhancing user engagement and expanding outreach through intelligent, data-driven solutions.

Dr. Elmeawad's educational journey is exemplary, holding two doctoral degrees that underscore her dedication to lifelong learning and her dual expertise in organizational leadership as well as information systems and technology. Her proficiency in AI has enabled her to integrate advanced machine learning algorithms and automation tools into library operations and educational initiatives, driving innovation and improving efficiency in information dissemination and user services.

Beyond her academic and professional accomplishments, Dr. Elmeawad is deeply committed to community service. As the Distinguished Lieutenant Governor for the Kiwanis Queens East Division, she leads community-focused initiatives that incorporate AI-driven strategies to address local challenges effectively. Her role as a board member of the KPTC further exemplifies her dedication to impactful community work, particularly in pediatric care and trauma prevention, where she utilizes AI to enhance service delivery and support systems.

Dr. Elmeawad's passion for mentorship and youth development is evident through her active involvement with the Benjamin Cardozo

High School Key Club. As a lead mentor, coach, and advisor, she guides young minds in their personal and professional growth by introducing them to the fundamentals of AI and its applications, fostering a new generation of leaders equipped with technological and ethical insights.

Her multifaceted expertise in artificial intelligence, coupled with her unwavering commitment to academic excellence and community service, makes Dr. Salwa Elmeawad a pioneering figure in her field and an inspiration to many. Her innovative approach to integrating AI in education and libraries not only advances these institutions but also empowers individuals and communities through enhanced access to knowledge and resources.

PREFACE

Libraries have long stood as beacons of knowledge, community engagement, and lifelong learning. Yet, in an era defined by rapid technological innovation, libraries face growing pressure to adapt and evolve. Artificial Intelligence (AI) offers both opportunities and challenges in this process of transformation opportunities to deepen engagement with patrons and enhance service delivery, and challenges to navigate the complexities of data privacy, ethics, and equity of access.

This book, *AI-Powered Libraries: A Practical Guide to Transforming Services and Operations*, was born out of a desire to help librarians, administrators, and stakeholders chart a clear path to AI adoption. Through our own experiences in libraries, research, and conversations with AI experts, we've seen firsthand how technology can greatly expand the reach and impact of library services. Yet we also understand that many library professionals grapple with the question, "Where do we begin?" This guide aims to answer that question and more laying out the foundational concepts of AI, examining real-world tools and their applications, offering a structured roadmap for implementation, and showcasing case studies that illustrate how AI can be put into practice successfully.

I have organized this book into four distinct parts. **Part I** lays the groundwork by defining AI and exploring its relevance in modern libraries. **Part II** delves into specific AI tools and technologies - from chatbots to intelligent recommendation systems - providing librarians with a practical toolkit for improving patron engagement and streamlining operations. **Part III** offers a step-by-step approach to planning, budgeting, piloting, and evaluating AI projects, ensuring that libraries can confidently integrate these new technologies at a pace that meets their unique needs. Finally, **Part IV** features case studies, ethical considerations, and future trends, giving you a holistic view of what AI can and should look like in the evolving library landscape.

Throughout this book, I emphasize responsible implementation and mindful innovation, encouraging libraries to adapt AI solutions that respect patron privacy and uphold equitable access to information. Our hope is that this guide will serve as both inspiration and a practical roadmap, enabling library professionals to not only adopt AI but to do so in a way that preserves the essential mission of libraries as inclusive, vibrant centers of community life.

I invite you to join us on this journey one that will shape the future of library services for generations to come.

Table of Contents

Vision for AI in Libraries

The integration of artificial intelligence (AI) into libraries represents a transformative shift in how these institutions envision their roles in a rapidly evolving digital age. AI-powered libraries aim to transcend traditional boundaries, leveraging cutting-edge technologies to enhance services, optimize operations, and redefine user engagement. This vision is not merely about adopting new tools; it's about fundamentally reimagining the library as a dynamic, adaptive, and forward-looking entity.

User-Centered Personalization

At the heart of the AI vision for libraries is the commitment to user-centered services. AI systems enable libraries to deliver personalized experiences, tailoring recommendations, resources, and services to individual users' needs and preferences. By analyzing user behavior, borrowing patterns, and search queries, libraries can proactively suggest relevant materials, programs, and learning opportunities. This personalization enhances user satisfaction and fosters a deeper connection between patrons and the library.

Enhanced Accessibility and Inclusion

AI technologies also empower libraries to become more inclusive and accessible. Natural language processing (NLP) tools can translate materials into multiple languages, making resources available to diverse communities. Text-to-speech and speech-to-text capabilities ensure that individuals with visual or hearing impairments can interact with library systems effectively. By embracing AI, libraries can break down barriers and ensure equitable access to knowledge for all.

Smart Operations and Resource Management

From the operational standpoint, AI offers unparalleled efficiency in resource management. Predictive analytics can forecast demand for specific materials, enabling libraries to optimize their acquisitions and reduce waste. Intelligent systems can automate cataloging, classification, and indexing, freeing librarians to focus on more strategic tasks. Furthermore, AI-powered chatbots and virtual assistants can handle routine inquiries, providing 24/7 support to users and streamlining library workflows.

Innovative Knowledge Discovery

AI's ability to analyze vast amounts of data opens new frontiers in knowledge discovery. Libraries can deploy machine learning algorithms to uncover hidden connections between resources, generating insights that might otherwise go unnoticed. These tools can support advanced research by enabling scholars to explore topics across disciplines, identifying trends and patterns in large datasets. By acting as hubs for cutting-edge AI-driven research tools, libraries position themselves as critical partners in innovation.

Strengthening Community Engagement

The vision for AI in libraries also includes fostering stronger ties with the community. AI-driven platforms can analyze community needs and preferences, informing program development and outreach initiatives. Virtual and augmented reality tools powered by AI can create immersive learning experiences, turning libraries into centers of experiential education. By staying attuned to community dynamics, libraries can remain relevant and responsive to the populations they serve.

Ethical Stewardship and Trust

As libraries integrate AI, they must uphold their longstanding commitment to ethical stewardship. Ensuring data privacy, combating algorithmic bias, and maintaining transparency in AI applications are essential aspects of this vision. Libraries are trusted institutions, and their use of AI must reinforce this trust by prioritizing fairness, inclusivity, and user autonomy.

Preparing for the Future

Finally, the vision for AI in libraries is about future-proofing these institutions. By embracing AI, libraries position themselves as leaders in the information ecosystem, adapting to changing user expectations and technological advancements. They become not just repositories of knowledge but also dynamic spaces for innovation, collaboration, and lifelong learning.

In summary, the vision for AI in libraries is one of transformation and empowerment. By integrating AI technologies thoughtfully and strategically, libraries can enhance their traditional roles while pioneering new ways to serve their communities, preserve knowledge, and inspire discovery in the digital age

Introduction

The Evolving Role of Libraries in the Age of AI

Libraries have long been at the forefront of knowledge preservation, dissemination, and community engagement. However, in the age of artificial intelligence (AI), their role is evolving to meet the demands of a digital and interconnected world. **AI-Powered Libraries: A Practical Guide to Transforming Services and Operations** explores how libraries can harness the potential of AI to redefine their services, enhance operational efficiency, and remain pivotal in society's intellectual and cultural fabric.

Libraries as Dynamic Information Hubs

Traditionally seen as repositories of physical books and resources, libraries have gradually transformed into dynamic information hubs, embracing digital media, online databases, and collaborative spaces. In the AI era, this transformation accelerates, positioning libraries as proactive, data-driven institutions capable of meeting diverse and rapidly changing user needs. AI offers tools to streamline processes, personalize user interactions, and analyze data at an unprecedented scale, allowing libraries to fulfill their missions in innovative ways.

Addressing the Challenges of a Digital World

The modern library operates in a landscape where information is abundant but often fragmented and overwhelming. With the rise of the internet, digital archives, and open-access platforms, users expect seamless access to relevant, high-quality resources. AI empowers libraries to meet these expectations by automating routine tasks, enabling advanced search capabilities, and curating tailored content. By adopting AI technologies, libraries can address the twin challenges of information overload and user engagement in a hyper-digital age.

15

Bridging the Gap Between Technology and Community

Libraries have always been community-centric institutions, fostering learning, cultural enrichment, and social inclusion. AI expands this role by offering tools that improve accessibility and inclusivity. For example, AI-driven language translation tools break down linguistic barriers, while adaptive technologies support patrons with disabilities. These capabilities enable libraries to serve as bridges between advanced technology and diverse populations, ensuring that no one is left behind in the digital transformation.

Redefining Librarianship

The integration of AI redefines the role of librarians as well. No longer confined to managing collections and assisting with resource navigation, librarians become curators of digital experiences and guides to the ethical use of AI tools. They act as facilitators, helping users navigate complex AI systems and extract meaningful insights. This shift in responsibilities highlights the importance of upskilling and professional development, ensuring that library staff are equipped to lead in this new era.

Libraries as Ethical Guardians

In the midst of AI's rapid adoption, libraries stand as ethical guardians, ensuring that technology is used responsibly. Libraries prioritize user privacy, data security, and equitable access to AI-driven resources. They play a critical role in addressing algorithmic bias, promoting transparency in AI applications, and educating users about the ethical implications of these technologies. This commitment reinforces libraries' position as trusted institutions in a time of rapid technological change.

A Vision of Transformation

The AI age offers libraries an opportunity to reimagine their purpose and value. By integrating AI, libraries can extend their reach, deepen their impact, and foster innovation. The transformation is not merely about technology adoption but about aligning services and operations with the evolving needs of their communities. AI-powered libraries embrace change while staying true to their core mission: to connect people with knowledge, support lifelong learning, and inspire curiosity.

In conclusion, the introduction of AI into libraries is not just a technical advancement but a paradigm shift. **AI-Powered Libraries: A Practical Guide to Transforming Services and Operations** serves as a roadmap for this transformation, offering actionable insights and strategies for libraries to thrive in the age of AI. It celebrates the enduring relevance of libraries while envisioning their future as adaptive, innovative, and indispensable institutions.

Why AI Matters for Libraries?

The rapid advancement of artificial intelligence (AI) has had transformative effects across industries, reshaping how services are delivered, operations are conducted, and communities are engaged. For libraries - long-standing institutions dedicated to knowledge dissemination and lifelong learning - AI represents an unprecedented opportunity to adapt to the evolving demands of the digital age. **AI-Powered Libraries: A Practical Guide to Transforming Services and Operations** examines why AI matters for libraries and how it can serve as a powerful catalyst for modernization and innovation.

Enhancing Service Delivery

Libraries exist to serve their communities, and AI offers tools to make that service delivery more efficient, personalized, and responsive. AI-powered systems can analyze user preferences, behaviors, and needs to deliver tailored recommendations, creating a more engaging and satisfying user experience. Whether it's suggesting relevant books, assisting with research queries, or providing adaptive learning tools, AI empowers libraries to meet individual users where they are, making their services more relevant and impactful.

Bridging the Accessibility Gap

Accessibility is a core value of libraries, and AI has the potential to bring this principle to new heights. AI technologies can break down barriers by providing real-time language translation, voice-to-text and text-to-voice applications, and adaptive interfaces for users with disabilities. These tools ensure that libraries remain inclusive spaces where everyone, regardless of their abilities or language proficiency, can access knowledge and resources.

Streamlining Operations

Behind the scenes, libraries require effective operations to manage their vast collections, systems, and workflows. AI simplifies and automates routine tasks such as cataloging, inventory management, and resource tagging. This not only increases operational efficiency but also allows library staff to focus on higher-value activities such as community engagement, programming, and innovative service development. AI-driven analytics also provide insights into user trends, helping libraries make data-informed decisions about acquisitions and programming.

Navigating the Information Explosion

In today's world, the volume of information available to users is overwhelming. Libraries play a critical role in helping users navigate this deluge of data. AI excels at organizing, filtering, and prioritizing vast amounts of information. Through advanced search capabilities, natural language processing (NLP), and machine learning, AI enables libraries to offer precise and contextually relevant results, ensuring that users can access high-quality and accurate information efficiently.

Supporting Lifelong Learning

Libraries are key enablers of lifelong learning, and AI aligns seamlessly with this mission. AI-powered tools such as adaptive learning platforms, virtual tutors, and immersive educational technologies enhance libraries' capacity to support education and skill development. By offering these advanced tools, libraries can empower users to acquire new knowledge, adapt to changing job markets, and pursue personal growth.

Fostering Innovation

AI positions libraries as hubs of innovation within their communities. Through initiatives such as makerspaces, AI labs, and access to AI-driven research tools, libraries can provide the resources and support for individuals and organizations to experiment, create, and innovate. These spaces encourage collaboration and exploration, cementing libraries' roles as centers for creativity and forward-thinking.

Preserving Ethical Standards

In an era where AI is reshaping society, libraries have a unique responsibility to ensure that these technologies are used ethically. Libraries are trusted institutions, and their integration of AI must uphold this trust by prioritizing transparency, data privacy, and fairness. Libraries can also educate users about the ethical implications of AI, providing workshops and resources on topics such as algorithmic bias, data security, and digital literacy.

Sustaining Relevance in a Digital Age

AI is not just a technological enhancement; it is a strategic necessity for libraries to remain relevant in a rapidly changing digital landscape. By embracing AI, libraries can redefine their value propositions, appeal to tech-savvy generations, and reaffirm their roles as indispensable community assets. AI ensures that libraries do not just survive but thrive in the digital age, continuing to inspire curiosity and connect people with knowledge.

In conclusion, AI matters for libraries because it aligns with their core mission while addressing the challenges and opportunities of a digital-first world. By integrating AI thoughtfully, libraries can transform their services and operations, ensuring they remain vital and adaptable institutions for generations to come. **AI-Powered Libraries: A Practical Guide to Transforming Services and Operations** provides the strategies and insights necessary to navigate this transformative journey, celebrating the enduring importance of libraries in an AI-driven future.

Part I: Foundations of AI in Libraries
Chapter 1: What Is AI?

Definition and Key Concepts

Artificial Intelligence (AI) refers to the simulation of human intelligence in machines designed to perform tasks that typically require human cognitive abilities. These tasks include learning, reasoning, problem-solving, understanding natural language, and perceiving and responding to the environment. In the context of libraries, AI encompasses a range of technologies that automate processes, analyze vast amounts of data, and enhance the delivery of information and services.

Understanding AI begins with an exploration of its foundational elements and key concepts, which are critical to grasping its applications in library settings.

1. Machine Learning (ML)

Machine Learning is a subset of AI focused on developing systems that learn and improve from experience without being explicitly programmed. In libraries, ML is integral to applications such as:

- **Recommendation Systems**: Suggesting books, articles, and resources based on user preferences and behavior patterns.

- **Predictive Analytics**: Anticipating trends, such as resource demand or foot traffic, to optimize library services and collections.

- **Automated Classification**: Enhancing cataloging processes by identifying patterns and categorizing resources more efficiently.

2. Natural Language Processing (NLP)

Natural Language Processing enables machines to understand, interpret, and respond to human language. NLP has significant implications for libraries, particularly in:

- **Search Optimization**: Enabling users to perform sophisticated and intuitive searches using everyday language.

- **Chatbots and Virtual Assistants**: Providing real-time support for common queries and guiding users through library services.

- **Text Analysis**: Analyzing the content of large datasets, such as historical documents, to uncover insights and patterns.

3. Computer Vision

Computer Vision is the ability of machines to interpret and process visual data, such as images and videos. In library contexts, computer vision can be used for:

- **Digitization Projects**: Automating the conversion of physical documents and manuscripts into searchable digital formats.

- **Object Recognition**: Identifying and cataloging resources based on their physical characteristics.

4. Robotics and Automation

AI-powered robotics enhance physical operations in libraries. Examples include:

- **Automated Shelving Systems**: Robots that organize and retrieve materials efficiently.

- **Service Robots**: Providing assistance, such as guiding users to specific sections or delivering requested items.

5. Data Analytics and Big Data

AI excels in processing and analyzing vast amounts of data, a capability that is highly valuable for libraries. Key applications include:

- **Usage Analysis**: Identifying patterns in resource usage to inform purchasing decisions.

- **Community Insights**: Understanding user demographics and behaviors to tailor programs and services.

- **Research Trends**: Highlighting emerging topics of interest to academic and research communities.

6. Artificial Neural Networks (ANNs)

Inspired by the human brain, ANNs are systems designed to recognize patterns and make predictions. Libraries can use neural networks for:

- **Optical Character Recognition (OCR)**: Converting scanned text into machine-readable formats.

- **Semantic Analysis**: Understanding relationships between concepts in large textual datasets.

7. Ethical AI

Ethical considerations are central to the use of AI in libraries. Libraries must ensure that AI applications are:

- **Transparent**: Clearly explaining how AI systems make decisions.

- **Fair and Unbiased**: Avoiding algorithmic bias that could disadvantage certain groups.

- **Privacy-Preserving**: Safeguarding user data and maintaining trust.

8. Human-AI Collaboration

AI does not replace the human expertise in libraries but enhances it. Librarians and staff work alongside AI tools to:

- **Enhance User Engagement**: Combining human insights with AI capabilities to provide personalized experiences.

- **Expand Service Offerings**: Utilizing AI to introduce innovative programs and services, such as AI literacy workshops.

- **Support Decision-Making**: Leveraging AI-driven data to inform strategic planning and resource allocation.

In conclusion, understanding the foundational elements of AI - its definition and key concepts - is essential for exploring its transformative potential in libraries. By integrating these technologies, libraries can enhance their services, streamline operations, and reinforce their roles as essential hubs of knowledge and innovation in the digital era. **AI-Powered Libraries: A Practical Guide to Transforming Services and Operations** offers a detailed exploration of these concepts, providing the groundwork for libraries to navigate and thrive in an AI-powered future.

Subfields of AI

Artificial Intelligence (AI) is a multifaceted field encompassing various subfields, each with its unique capabilities and applications. These subfields work together to enable machines to simulate human-like intelligence and perform complex tasks. For libraries, understanding these subfields is crucial to harnessing AI effectively to enhance services and streamline operations. Below are the key subfields of AI and their relevance to library environments:

1. Machine Learning (ML)

Machine Learning is the backbone of many AI applications. It involves algorithms that enable systems to learn from data and improve their performance over time without explicit programming.

Applications in Libraries:

o **Recommendation Engines**: Suggesting books, journals, and other materials based on user history and preferences.

o **Predictive Analytics**: Anticipating demand for specific resources or identifying seasonal trends in usage.

o **Automated Classification**: Grouping and categorizing library resources more accurately and efficiently.

o **User Behavior Analysis**: Understanding patron needs and improving service personalization.

2. Natural Language Processing (NLP)

Natural Language Processing focuses on the interaction between computers and human language, enabling machines to understand, interpret, and generate text and speech.

Applications in Libraries:

o **Enhanced Search Capabilities**: Allowing users to search library catalogs using conversational language or questions.

o **Chatbots and Virtual Assistants**: Offering real-time assistance for common queries, guiding users to resources, and providing information about library services.

o **Text Summarization**: Condensing long documents into concise summaries to aid quick understanding.

o **Language Translation**: Making resources accessible to non-native speakers and multilingual communities.

3. Computer Vision

Computer Vision enables machines to interpret and analyze visual data, such as images and videos. It mimics human vision but with enhanced capabilities to process and recognize patterns.

Applications in Libraries:

o **Digitization Projects**: Automating the scanning and conversion of physical documents, manuscripts, and historical archives into digital formats.

o **Optical Character Recognition (OCR)**: Extracting text from scanned documents to create searchable databases.

o **Image Cataloging**: Classifying and tagging visual materials like photographs, illustrations, and videos for easier retrieval.

o **Real-Time Monitoring**: Enhancing security and tracking resource usage within library spaces.

4. Robotics and Automation

This subfield involves the use of robots and automated systems to perform tasks traditionally done by humans.

Applications in Libraries:

o **Automated Shelving and Retrieval Systems**: Robots that organize, retrieve, and restock materials efficiently.

o **Self-Checkout Kiosks**: Enhancing user convenience and reducing wait times.

o **Service Robots**: Providing assistance in navigating library spaces or answering basic queries.

5. Data Analytics and Big Data

AI's ability to process and analyze large datasets quickly and accurately is crucial for extracting meaningful insights.

Applications in Libraries:

o **User Trend Analysis**: Identifying patterns in borrowing, attendance, and program participation to inform service improvements.

o **Resource Optimization**: Helping libraries allocate budgets and space based on user preferences and resource popularity.

o **Impact Measurement**: Analyzing data to evaluate the effectiveness of library initiatives and programs.

6. Artificial Neural Networks (ANNs)

ANNs are computational models inspired by the structure of the human brain. They are designed to recognize patterns, make predictions, and perform complex problem-solving.

Applications in Libraries:

o **Semantic Analysis**: Understanding relationships between topics and concepts in vast collections of text.

o **Automated Decision-Making**: Supporting librarians in acquisition decisions by predicting future resource demand.

o **Content Curation**: Identifying thematic connections between disparate resources for improved discovery.

7. Speech Recognition and Synthesis

This subfield enables machines to understand spoken language (speech recognition) and generate human-like speech (synthesis).

Applications in Libraries:

o **Voice-Activated Search**: Allowing patrons to search catalogs using voice commands.

o **Accessibility Enhancements**: Supporting users with visual impairments through text-to-speech applications.

o **Multilingual Interfaces**: Providing spoken translations and voice guidance in multiple languages.

8. Ethical AI and Responsible Design

This emerging subfield ensures that AI systems are designed and implemented responsibly, adhering to principles of fairness, transparency, and accountability.

Applications in Libraries:

o **Data Privacy**: Ensuring that patron data collected by AI systems is secure and used ethically.

o **Bias Mitigation**: Addressing and minimizing biases in AI algorithms to promote inclusivity.

o **AI Literacy Programs**: Educating library users about ethical AI use and its societal implications.

In summary, the subfields of AI provide libraries with a toolkit of technologies to enhance operations and elevate user experiences. By understanding and integrating these subfields, libraries can not only optimize their current services but also innovate and adapt to the changing needs of their communities. **AI-Powered Libraries: A Practical Guide to Transforming Services and Operations** serves as a comprehensive resource to explore these subfields and their transformative potential for modern libraries.

Ethical Implications of AI

The adoption of artificial intelligence (AI) in libraries is a powerful step toward enhancing services and optimizing operations. However, as with any transformative technology, its implementation comes with significant ethical considerations. Libraries have long been regarded as trusted institutions that uphold principles of fairness, equity, and privacy. These values must be preserved as AI becomes integrated into their operations. Addressing the ethical implications of AI is critical to ensuring its responsible and sustainable use in libraries.

1. Data Privacy and Security

AI systems often rely on vast amounts of data to function effectively. In libraries, this may include user information, borrowing habits, and search histories.

Challenges:

o   Ensuring that sensitive patron data is protected against breaches or unauthorized access.

o   Avoiding the misuse of personal data for purposes beyond library services.

Ethical Practices:

o   Implementing robust encryption and data protection measures.

o   Clearly communicating data collection and usage policies to users.

o   Offering patrons control over their data, including options to opt out of data collection.

2. Algorithmic Bias

AI systems are only as unbiased as the data they are trained on. If training data reflects societal biases, these biases can be perpetuated or amplified in AI outcomes.

Challenges:

o   Risk of underrepresentation or misrepresentation of marginalized groups in library AI systems.

o   Potential for AI recommendations or search results to favor certain perspectives or resources over others.

Ethical Practices:

o   Regularly auditing AI systems for bias and ensuring diverse datasets are used for training.

o   Incorporating inclusive design principles to represent all community members fairly.

o   Engaging diverse stakeholders in the development and evaluation of AI tools.

3. Transparency and Explainability

AI often operates as a "black box," where its decision-making processes are not immediately understandable to users or even developers.

Challenges:

o   Lack of clarity about how AI systems make recommendations or decisions, potentially eroding trust.

o   Difficulty in addressing errors or unexpected outcomes in opaque systems.

Ethical Practices:

o   Prioritizing the use of interpretable AI models and tools.

o   Clearly explaining how AI systems work and what factors influence their decisions.

o   Providing channels for users to challenge or seek clarification on AI-driven decisions.

4. Equity and Accessibility

AI has the potential to democratize access to knowledge, but it can also inadvertently exclude certain groups if not designed inclusively.

Challenges:

o   Risk of creating barriers for users without digital literacy skills or access to technology.

o   Potential for AI interfaces to overlook the needs of individuals with disabilities or those speaking minority languages.

Ethical Practices:

o   Ensuring that AI-driven services are accessible to all, including those with disabilities.

o   Designing interfaces and systems that are user-friendly and intuitive for diverse populations.

o   Supporting AI literacy initiatives to empower users to navigate and utilize AI tools effectively.

5. Intellectual Freedom and Censorship

AI systems play a role in curating and recommending content. However, they may inadvertently filter out certain viewpoints or restrict access to certain materials.

Challenges:

o   Risk of "filter bubbles," where users are only exposed to information aligned with their preferences or past behaviors.

o   Potential for AI algorithms to prioritize popular content at the expense of niche or critical works.

Ethical Practices:

o   Ensuring that AI systems promote intellectual freedom by exposing users to diverse perspectives and resources.

o   Regularly evaluating AI algorithms to prevent inadvertent censorship or skewing of information.

o   Balancing algorithmic recommendations with human oversight to ensure diverse content representation.

6. Job Displacement and Workforce Impact

As AI automates routine tasks, concerns about its impact on library staff arise.

Challenges:

o   Risk of reducing roles or responsibilities traditionally performed by library personnel.

o   Potential loss of human touch in library services.

Ethical Practices:

o   Using AI to augment rather than replace human expertise, allowing staff to focus on more strategic and creative tasks.

o   Investing in professional development and upskilling for library staff to adapt to AI-enhanced roles.

o   Preserving human-centered interactions alongside AI-driven automation.

7. Ethical Education and Advocacy

Libraries serve as educators and advocates for their communities. In the AI era, this responsibility extends to informing users about the ethical implications of AI.

Ethical Practices:

o   Hosting workshops and discussions on AI ethics, including topics like algorithmic bias, data privacy, and digital literacy.

o   Providing resources and guidance for users to critically evaluate AI-driven tools and information.

o   Advocating for ethical AI practices in broader societal contexts, leveraging libraries' roles as trusted community hubs.

In conclusion, while AI offers immense opportunities for libraries to enhance their services, these benefits must be balanced with a thoughtful approach to ethics. Addressing concerns around privacy, bias, transparency, and equity ensures that AI remains a force for good within library systems. By adopting ethical practices and fostering a culture of accountability, libraries can maintain their longstanding commitment to serving as equitable, inclusive, and trustworthy institutions in the age of AI.

Chapter 2: The Changing Landscape of Library Services

Traditional vs. Digital-Era Library Services

The role of libraries has evolved dramatically over time, shifting from traditional service models to those designed for a digital era. This evolution reflects broader societal and technological changes, with artificial intelligence (AI) playing a pivotal role in transforming library operations and services. Understanding the contrasts between traditional and digital-era library services highlights the profound impact AI has in reshaping these institutions.

Traditional Library Services

Historically, libraries have served as custodians of physical knowledge, focusing on providing access to books, periodicals, and other tangible resources. Key characteristics of traditional library services include:

1. **Physical Collections**:

o   Libraries maintained extensive shelves of books, journals, and archival materials.

o   Users needed to visit libraries in person to access resources.

2. **Manual Cataloging and Retrieval**:

o   Library staff were responsible for cataloging and indexing materials, often using card catalogs or early computer systems.

o   Users relied on librarians to locate specific resources.

3. **One-Size-Fits-All Services**:

o   Programs and services catered to general audiences, with limited capacity for personalization.

o Recommendations and assistance were typically provided face-to-face.

4. **Community Hubs**:

o Libraries functioned as spaces for quiet study, reading, and accessing limited educational programming.

o Interactions were predominantly physical and localized.

5. **Static Information Flow**:

o Information was presented in a linear format, often requiring users to sift through resources manually.

Digital-Era Library Services

In the digital age, libraries have expanded their scope to incorporate digital resources, online access, and AI-powered tools. This shift has revolutionized how services are delivered, making libraries more accessible, efficient, and personalized.

1. **Hybrid Collections**:

o Libraries now provide access to both physical and digital collections, including eBooks, audiobooks, databases, and multimedia resources.

o Remote access enables users to interact with resources anytime, anywhere.

2. **Automated Cataloging and Discovery**:

o AI streamlines cataloging and indexing, making resources more discoverable through advanced search algorithms.

o Users can search catalogs using natural language or voice commands, retrieving results instantly.

3. **Personalized User Experiences**:

o AI analyzes user behavior to deliver tailored recommendations for books, articles, and programs.

o Adaptive learning platforms support individual educational journeys.

4. **Global Connectivity**:

o Libraries now serve as gateways to global information networks, connecting users to knowledge and communities worldwide.

o Virtual programs and AI-driven chatbots enable engagement beyond physical boundaries.

5. **Dynamic Information Flow**:

o AI systems facilitate real-time updates, semantic analysis, and dynamic content curation, making information more accessible and relevant.

Key Shifts from Traditional to Digital-Era Services

1. **Access vs. Engagement**:

o Traditional libraries focused on providing access to static collections; digital-era libraries emphasize user engagement through interactive and AI-enhanced services.

2. **Local vs. Global Reach**:

o Physical libraries primarily served local communities; digital libraries extend their reach globally, transcending geographical boundaries.

3. **Manual vs. Automated Operations**:

o   Manual processes dominated traditional libraries; automation and AI have streamlined operations, enabling libraries to handle larger volumes of resources and users.

4. **Generalized vs. Personalized Services**:

o   Traditional services were one-size-fits-all; AI allows for highly personalized user experiences, catering to individual preferences and needs.

5. **Static vs. Dynamic Knowledge Ecosystems**:

o   Information in traditional libraries was static and localized; digital libraries operate within dynamic ecosystems, providing real-time updates and connections across disciplines.

The Role of AI in Bridging the Gap

AI serves as the transformative force enabling libraries to transition from traditional to digital-era service models. By automating routine tasks, personalizing user interactions, and integrating advanced technologies, AI empowers libraries to:

• Expand their resource offerings without overwhelming staff.

• Deliver services that meet modern users' expectations for convenience, speed, and customization.

• Preserve the core values of libraries—access to knowledge, community enrichment, and inclusivity—while adapting to a digital-first world.

In conclusion, the transition from traditional to digital-era library services underscores the profound impact of technological advancements, particularly AI, on library operations. By embracing these changes, libraries can maintain their relevance and continue to serve as essential community resources in a rapidly evolving information landscape.

How Patrons' Expectations Are Evolving

As technology reshapes nearly every aspect of modern life, patrons' expectations of libraries are evolving rapidly. In an era dominated by digital connectivity, instant access to information, and personalized experiences, libraries must adapt to remain relevant and impactful. Artificial intelligence (AI) plays a pivotal role in meeting these shifting demands, allowing libraries to deliver services aligned with patrons' growing expectations for convenience, efficiency, and engagement.

1. Instantaneous Access to Information

In the digital age, patrons are accustomed to on-demand access to information and services. The prevalence of search engines, streaming platforms, and e-commerce has set new benchmarks for immediacy.

- **Expectations**:
  o Rapid access to library catalogs and resources without the need for manual searches.

  o Digital resources, such as eBooks and academic journals, available 24/7.

- **AI Solutions**:
  o Intelligent search algorithms that quickly locate relevant materials.

  o Virtual assistants and chatbots capable of addressing queries in real-time.

  o Automated delivery of digital resources through seamless platforms.

2. Personalized Experiences

Modern consumers expect tailored recommendations and interactions, a trend driven by AI-powered platforms like Netflix and Amazon. This expectation extends to library services.

- **Expectations**:

o Personalized reading recommendations based on borrowing history and preferences.

o Curated content for academic or professional pursuits.

- **AI Solutions**:

o Machine learning algorithms that analyze user behavior to generate tailored suggestions.

o Adaptive learning tools that adjust to individual users' educational needs and goals.

o Dynamic resource alerts based on patrons' past interests and interactions.

3. Accessibility and Inclusivity

With greater awareness of diversity and inclusion, patrons now expect libraries to be accessible to all, regardless of physical, linguistic, or technological barriers.

- **Expectations**:

o Resources available in multiple languages.

o Tools that cater to patrons with disabilities, such as screen readers or voice commands.

- **AI Solutions**:

o Natural Language Processing (NLP) tools for real-time language translation.

o Text-to-speech and speech-to-text technologies for visually or hearing-impaired users.

o Adaptive user interfaces that provide equitable access to library systems.

4. Seamless Digital Integration

Patrons increasingly expect libraries to integrate seamlessly with the digital ecosystems they use daily, such as mobile apps, online databases, and cloud-based platforms.

- **Expectations**:

o Mobile-friendly access to library resources and services.

o Synchronization of library accounts with external educational and research tools.

- **AI Solutions**:

o Mobile apps powered by AI for resource browsing, reservations, and notifications.

o Cloud-based platforms that facilitate integration with external tools like citation managers or collaborative research platforms.

o AI-driven digital assistants embedded into existing library apps for streamlined access.

5. Active Learning and Engagement

Patrons no longer view libraries solely as repositories of knowledge; they seek active engagement and experiential learning opportunities.

- **Expectations**:

o Interactive and immersive learning experiences.

o Opportunities to engage with cutting-edge technologies, such as AI and VR.

- **AI Solutions**:

o AI-driven tools for interactive educational programs, such as virtual tutors or language learning platforms.

o Integration of augmented and virtual reality for immersive experiences in history, science, and the arts.

o Predictive analytics to design programs and workshops aligned with emerging community interests.

6. Ethical and Transparent Practices

With the increased use of technology, patrons expect libraries to uphold high ethical standards, particularly concerning data privacy and algorithmic transparency.

- **Expectations**:

o Assurance that personal data is secure and used responsibly.

o Clear communication about how AI-driven systems make decisions or recommendations.

- **AI Solutions**:

o Privacy-focused AI designs that prioritize user consent and data security.

o Transparent algorithms that allow users to understand the logic behind recommendations.

o Educational initiatives to inform patrons about AI technologies and their ethical implications.

7. Community-Centric Roles

Patrons increasingly view libraries as vital community hubs that foster collaboration, social engagement, and collective growth.

- **Expectations**:

- o Programs that address community-specific needs, such as career development or digital literacy.

- o Platforms for collaboration and connection among community members.

- **AI Solutions**:

- o AI analytics to identify and address community trends, ensuring relevant programming.

- o Virtual collaboration tools powered by AI to facilitate group projects and networking.

- o AI-enhanced outreach efforts to engage underrepresented or underserved populations.

8. Continuous Innovation

Patrons expect libraries to remain at the forefront of technological advancements, offering access to cutting-edge tools and staying relevant in a rapidly changing digital landscape.

- **Expectations**:

- o Exposure to emerging technologies like AI, robotics, and machine learning.

- o Opportunities to learn about and experiment with new tech in a supportive environment.

- **AI Solutions**:

- o Makerspaces and AI labs for patrons to explore and innovate with advanced tools.

- o Workshops on AI literacy, coding, and technology applications for various industries.

o   AI-powered content creation tools to support patrons in creative and professional endeavors.

In conclusion, patrons' expectations are shifting toward greater convenience, personalization, inclusivity, and innovation. Libraries must evolve to meet these demands, leveraging AI to bridge the gap between traditional values and modern technological possibilities. By addressing these evolving expectations, libraries not only maintain their relevance but also reaffirm their commitment to serving as dynamic, forward-thinking institutions in an increasingly digital world.

The Role of AI in Meeting Modern Information Needs

The emergence of artificial intelligence (AI) has significantly transformed how libraries meet the modern information needs of their patrons. In an era characterized by the exponential growth of digital content, diverse user expectations, and the demand for instant and personalized access to knowledge, AI provides the tools and strategies necessary for libraries to adapt. By automating processes, enhancing search capabilities, and enabling personalized services, AI is reshaping the role of libraries as essential hubs for information in the digital age.

1. Managing the Information Overload

The digital era has brought an overwhelming volume of information, making it challenging for users to locate relevant and credible resources. Libraries, traditionally seen as curators of knowledge, now face the task of organizing and filtering vast datasets.

How AI Helps:

o   **Advanced Search and Discovery**: AI-powered search engines use natural language processing (NLP) and semantic analysis to provide precise and contextually relevant results.

- o **Automated Content Curation**: Machine learning algorithms analyze user preferences and recommend materials that align with their interests, reducing the time spent searching.

- o **Data Visualization**: AI tools transform complex datasets into visual formats, making it easier for users to interpret and utilize information.

2. Enhancing Research Capabilities

Modern research demands tools that go beyond traditional bibliographic searches, offering advanced insights and connections across disciplines.

How AI Helps:

- o **Pattern Recognition**: AI identifies patterns and trends in large datasets, enabling researchers to uncover hidden connections between ideas or topics.

- o **Text Mining and Analysis**: Tools powered by AI extract key insights from unstructured data, such as journal articles or historical documents, aiding scholarly work.

- o **Citation Analysis**: AI tracks and predicts citation trends, helping users understand the impact and relevance of specific works.

3. Personalizing User Experiences

In an age where personalization drives user engagement, libraries must cater to the unique needs and preferences of their patrons.

How AI Helps:

- o **Customized Recommendations**: AI analyzes borrowing histories, search behavior, and preferences to suggest books, articles, or programs tailored to individual users.

o **Adaptive Learning Platforms**: AI adjusts educational resources to match a user's skill level and learning pace, enhancing their experience.

o **Dynamic Notifications**: Users receive alerts about new arrivals, events, or resources that align with their interests.

4. Increasing Accessibility and Inclusivity

Libraries serve diverse communities, including individuals with disabilities, non-native speakers, and those with varying levels of digital literacy.

How AI Helps:

o **Language Translation**: AI-driven NLP tools provide real-time translation of materials, making resources accessible to multilingual audiences.

o **Assistive Technologies**: AI enables text-to-speech, speech-to-text, and image recognition tools to support users with visual or hearing impairments.

o **Simplified Interfaces**: User-friendly, AI-powered systems cater to individuals with limited technological skills, ensuring equitable access.

5. Automating Routine Operations

Libraries face growing demands with limited resources, making operational efficiency critical to meeting user needs.

How AI Helps:

o **Automated Cataloging**: AI streamlines the classification and indexing of new materials, reducing the workload on library staff.

o **Self-Service Systems**: AI-powered kiosks and chatbots handle routine queries, freeing librarians to focus on more complex tasks.

- o **Predictive Resource Management**: AI forecasts demand for specific materials, optimizing inventory and acquisition strategies.

6. Enabling Collaborative Knowledge Creation

Modern libraries are not just centers for information retrieval but also platforms for collaboration and innovation.

How AI Helps:

- o **Collaborative Tools**: AI integrates with platforms that allow users to work together on projects, share resources, and co-create knowledge.

- o **Virtual Makerspaces**: Libraries can offer AI-driven environments for patrons to experiment with emerging technologies, fostering creativity and innovation.

- o **Community Insights**: AI analyzes user trends to design programs that address the collective needs and interests of the library's community.

7. Addressing the Need for Ethical and Reliable Information

The proliferation of misinformation and biased algorithms presents significant challenges in the digital age. Libraries play a vital role in promoting critical thinking and reliable information.

How AI Helps:

- o **Content Verification**: AI tools detect and flag misinformation, ensuring patrons access credible and accurate resources.

- o **Algorithmic Transparency**: Libraries can adopt AI systems that explain their decision-making processes, fostering trust and accountability.

- o **AI Literacy Programs**: Educating patrons about how AI works and its implications, empowering them to navigate digital information responsibly.

8. Future-Proofing Library Services

As technology evolves, so do the expectations of library patrons. AI ensures that libraries remain adaptable and forward-thinking institutions capable of meeting future information needs.

How AI Helps:

o **Continuous Learning Systems**: AI adapts to emerging trends, updating library systems and services to remain relevant.

o **Proactive Engagement**: AI identifies shifting user needs and recommends innovations to address them.

o **Integration with Emerging Technologies**: AI serves as a foundation for incorporating tools like augmented reality (AR), virtual reality (VR), and blockchain into library services.

In conclusion, AI is revolutionizing how libraries meet the modern information needs of their patrons. By enhancing search capabilities, personalizing experiences, and improving accessibility, AI empowers libraries to remain essential resources in the digital age. Through thoughtful integration and ethical implementation, libraries can use AI to uphold their mission of connecting people with knowledge while adapting to the changing landscape of information and technology.

Chapter 3: AI in the Wider Context of Education and Research

AI's Impact on Learning and Research

Artificial intelligence (AI) is revolutionizing education and research, redefining how knowledge is created, disseminated, and consumed. For libraries, which serve as critical bridges between educational institutions, researchers, and the broader community, AI presents unparalleled opportunities to enhance learning and research. From personalizing education to streamlining scholarly inquiry, AI's impact on these domains is profound and transformative.

1. Personalization of Learning Experiences

AI has made personalized learning a reality, catering to individual preferences, learning styles, and paces.

How AI Enhances Learning:

o **Adaptive Learning Platforms**: AI-powered tools tailor educational content based on a learner's performance and knowledge gaps, ensuring a more effective learning experience.

o **Customized Recommendations**: Libraries can leverage AI to suggest resources—books, articles, or multimedia—that align with a student's academic goals or interests.

o **Dynamic Assessments**: AI can provide real-time feedback and adaptive quizzes that evolve with the learner's progress, helping them master complex subjects.

Benefits for Libraries:

o Supporting educators by offering AI-driven tools for lesson planning and resource curation.

o Helping lifelong learners discover content that matches their personal and professional aspirations.

2. Facilitating Multidisciplinary Research

Modern research increasingly spans multiple disciplines, requiring tools that can synthesize diverse datasets and generate meaningful insights.

How AI Advances Research:

o **Data Integration**: AI systems aggregate and analyze data from various sources, uncovering connections across disciplines that might otherwise be overlooked.

o **Pattern Recognition**: Machine learning algorithms identify trends and patterns in research data, aiding discoveries in areas like medicine, climate science, and engineering.

o **Semantic Analysis**: AI can parse through millions of articles, linking related concepts and fostering cross-disciplinary collaboration.

Benefits for Libraries:

o Providing researchers with AI-powered tools that streamline literature reviews and identify seminal works.

o Acting as hubs for interdisciplinary collaboration by offering platforms that merge AI with domain-specific expertise.

3. Enhancing Accessibility and Inclusivity in Education

AI democratizes education by breaking down barriers to learning, ensuring that resources are accessible to all.

How AI Promotes Inclusion:

o **Real-Time Translation**: AI-driven translation tools enable access to educational materials in multiple languages.

o **Assistive Technologies**: Tools like text-to-speech and speech-to-text cater to individuals with visual or auditory impairments, making learning more inclusive.

o **Universal Design for Learning**: AI-powered systems adapt interfaces and content to meet diverse learners' needs, including those with disabilities.

Benefits for Libraries:

o Extending access to global educational resources, ensuring equity for all patrons.

o Offering AI tools that support underserved populations and promote digital literacy.

4. Automating Scholarly Workflows

The research process often involves repetitive tasks that can be streamlined through AI, allowing scholars to focus on innovation and critical thinking.

How AI Supports Researchers:

o **Literature Mining**: AI algorithms sift through vast bibliographies, summarizing key findings and identifying relevant citations.

o **Data Analysis**: AI simplifies complex statistical computations and visualizations, accelerating the pace of research.

o **Research Management**: Tools powered by AI assist in organizing references, drafting proposals, and formatting manuscripts.

Benefits for Libraries:

o Offering services that integrate AI into research workflows, reducing time spent on administrative tasks.

o Supporting reproducibility by providing AI systems that manage and analyze research datasets.

5. Enabling Collaborative and Global Education

AI fosters collaboration among students, educators, and researchers by connecting individuals and institutions across the globe.

How AI Drives Collaboration:

o **Virtual Learning Environments**: AI powers platforms where students and educators can interact, collaborate, and share resources in real-time, irrespective of geographical barriers.

o **Global Research Networks**: AI links researchers with similar interests, enabling partnerships and joint projects across continents.

o **Crowdsourced Knowledge**: AI facilitates the sharing of data, insights, and resources, creating a global repository of collective intelligence.

Benefits for Libraries:

o Hosting AI-driven platforms for collaborative research and educational projects.

o Offering tools for virtual workshops, conferences, and knowledge-sharing sessions.

6. Supporting Ethical Research and Education

AI not only accelerates learning and research but also raises critical questions about ethics, data privacy, and equity in these fields.

How AI Ensures Ethical Practices:

o **Bias Detection**: AI systems can identify and address biases in datasets, ensuring fairness in educational and research outcomes.

o **Data Integrity**: AI tools enhance data management practices, ensuring accuracy and accountability in research.

o **Critical AI Literacy**: Libraries and educational institutions can use AI to teach students and researchers about the ethical implications of its use.

Benefits for Libraries:

o Acting as stewards of ethical AI by promoting transparency and equity in its applications.

o Offering workshops and resources that educate patrons on responsible AI usage in academic and professional contexts.

7. Future-Proofing Education and Research

AI equips libraries and educational institutions to adapt to future challenges, ensuring they remain at the forefront of knowledge dissemination and innovation.

How AI Prepares for the Future:

o **Predictive Insights**: AI systems analyze emerging trends, helping institutions anticipate and prepare for future educational needs.

o **Scalable Solutions**: AI-powered tools accommodate growing student populations and research demands without compromising quality.

o **Integration with Emerging Technologies**: AI serves as a foundation for incorporating innovations like augmented reality (AR), virtual reality (VR), and quantum computing into education and research.

Benefits for Libraries:

o Offering cutting-edge AI tools that align with evolving educational and research paradigms.

o   Positioning libraries as leaders in driving innovation within academic and research ecosystems.

In conclusion, AI's impact on learning and research is profound, providing tools and strategies that enhance personalization, inclusivity, collaboration, and innovation. Libraries play a pivotal role in integrating AI into these domains, serving as enablers of knowledge and stewards of ethical practices. By embracing AI, libraries ensure that they remain indispensable partners in education and research, meeting the demands of a rapidly changing world.

Collaborative Opportunities with Educational Institutions

Artificial intelligence (AI) has created new avenues for collaboration between libraries and educational institutions. By integrating their resources, expertise, and technology, libraries and schools, colleges, and universities can form symbiotic partnerships that enhance learning, streamline research, and create innovative educational experiences. Libraries equipped with AI tools become not just resource providers but active collaborators in the broader educational ecosystem.

1. Enhancing Curriculum Development

Libraries, with their wealth of resources and expertise in knowledge organization, can play a pivotal role in shaping educational curricula that leverage AI.

Collaborative Opportunities:

o   **Curriculum Support**: Libraries provide access to AI-powered research tools and resources that educators can use to develop engaging and up-to-date course materials.

o   **AI Integration in Learning**: Partnering with institutions to create AI-focused programs, such as courses on data science, natural language processing, or ethical AI.

- **Content Recommendations**: AI in libraries can analyze curriculum requirements and suggest relevant books, articles, and multimedia resources.

2. Joint Research Initiatives

AI offers advanced tools for research, enabling libraries and educational institutions to work together on scholarly projects and innovations.

Collaborative Opportunities:

- **Data-Driven Research**: Libraries provide access to AI systems that analyze large datasets, enabling researchers to uncover trends, connections, and insights.

- **Interdisciplinary Collaboration**: Libraries serve as hubs for interdisciplinary research, connecting faculty and students from different departments using AI tools to bridge diverse academic fields.

- **Grant Proposals**: Partnering with educational institutions to apply for grants aimed at integrating AI into research infrastructure.

3. Supporting Lifelong Learning

Educational institutions are increasingly embracing the concept of lifelong learning, and libraries are natural allies in this endeavor.

Collaborative Opportunities:

- **Continuing Education Programs**: Libraries and institutions can co-host workshops, certifications, and seminars on AI-related topics, ensuring the workforce remains competitive in a rapidly evolving job market.

o **Professional Development**: Collaborating to offer faculty and staff training on AI tools and their applications in teaching and research.

o **Public Engagement**: Creating community programs that introduce AI literacy to non-traditional learners, ensuring equitable access to cutting-edge knowledge.

4. Shared Technological Resources

AI technologies often require substantial investment, and partnerships can help libraries and institutions share the costs and benefits of these tools.

Collaborative Opportunities:

o **AI Labs and Makerspaces**: Establishing shared facilities where students, educators, and library patrons can experiment with AI-driven technologies, such as machine learning models or robotics.

o **Resource Access**: Offering institutional access to library-owned AI platforms, such as research analytics tools or adaptive learning systems.

o **Cloud-Based Platforms**: Jointly developing and maintaining cloud-based AI solutions to enhance accessibility and reduce redundancy.

5. Fostering Innovation and Creativity

Libraries and educational institutions can leverage AI to create environments that encourage experimentation, creativity, and entrepreneurship.

Collaborative Opportunities:

o **Hackathons and Innovation Challenges**: Co-hosting events where students and researchers solve real-world problems using AI technologies.

o **AI-Powered Content Creation**: Libraries can offer tools for producing multimedia content, such as video editing powered by AI or automated transcription services for academic projects.

o **Knowledge Hubs**: Establishing knowledge-sharing platforms that use AI to curate and recommend resources for innovation-focused initiatives.

6. Promoting Ethical AI Practices

The widespread adoption of AI necessitates a focus on ethical considerations, and libraries can collaborate with educational institutions to champion responsible AI use.

Collaborative Opportunities:

o **Ethics Workshops**: Co-developing programs that teach students and faculty about algorithmic bias, data privacy, and the societal impact of AI.

o **Policy Development**: Partnering to create guidelines for the ethical use of AI in education and research, ensuring fairness and transparency.

o **Community Advocacy**: Libraries and institutions can jointly engage with the public to build awareness about AI ethics and its implications for society.

7. Expanding Access and Equity

Collaboration between libraries and educational institutions can address disparities in access to technology and information, ensuring inclusivity in AI-powered initiatives.

Collaborative Opportunities:

o **Digital Inclusion Programs**: Libraries can work with schools to provide underserved communities with access to AI-driven tools and training.

- o **Resource Sharing**: Educational institutions can partner with libraries to extend digital resource access to non-enrolled learners, such as alumni or local community members.

- o **Localized Solutions**: Using AI to analyze community needs and create targeted programs addressing specific educational gaps.

8. Enhancing Student Engagement

AI-driven tools can create more engaging and interactive learning experiences, and libraries are well-positioned to support this goal.

Collaborative Opportunities:

- o **Gamification**: Using AI to develop educational games and simulations hosted in libraries, enhancing student learning and engagement.

- o **Virtual Reality Integration**: Libraries and institutions can collaborate to offer immersive VR experiences powered by AI for exploring historical events, scientific phenomena, or artistic creations.

- o **Real-Time Feedback Systems**: AI-enabled feedback tools, accessible through libraries, can help students refine their learning strategies.

9. Preparing for the Future

Libraries and educational institutions can work together to future-proof their systems and services, ensuring relevance in an AI-driven world.

Collaborative Opportunities:

- o **Strategic Planning**: Jointly designing roadmaps for the adoption of AI in teaching, research, and library services.

- o **Workforce Readiness**: Preparing students for AI-integrated careers through exposure to tools and technologies in library settings.

- o **Integration of Emerging Technologies**: Partnering to explore and implement technologies like augmented reality (AR), blockchain, and quantum computing in education.

In conclusion, the collaborative opportunities between libraries and educational institutions are vast and impactful. By integrating their expertise, resources, and goals, these partnerships can leverage AI to enhance learning, drive research, and foster innovation. Libraries, as trusted and dynamic institutions, play a central role in these collaborations, ensuring that AI is used ethically, inclusively, and effectively.

Future Trends and Emerging Technologies

The rapid evolution of artificial intelligence (AI) continues to reshape the landscape of education and research, presenting libraries with transformative opportunities. Future trends and emerging technologies are poised to further enhance the integration of AI in libraries, enabling these institutions to remain at the forefront of knowledge dissemination and innovation. By embracing these advancements, libraries can redefine their roles as critical hubs for lifelong learning, research, and collaboration.

1. AI-Driven Knowledge Graphs

AI-powered knowledge graphs are revolutionizing how information is organized, connected, and accessed. These systems map relationships between concepts, enabling deeper exploration of interconnected topics.

Future Applications:

- o Libraries can offer intuitive and visual tools that help patrons understand complex relationships across disciplines.

o Researchers can identify novel connections and gaps in existing literature, fostering innovative inquiries.

o Knowledge graphs can power personalized recommendations based on a patron's area of interest or research focus.

2. Immersive Learning with Augmented and Virtual Reality

AR and VR technologies, integrated with AI, are redefining educational experiences by creating immersive and interactive environments.

Future Applications:

o Libraries can host virtual labs where users explore scientific phenomena, historical events, or artistic works in a 3D space.

o AI can personalize VR learning paths based on a user's preferences and learning style.

o AR-enhanced physical collections can provide real-time, interactive information overlays, blending the physical and digital worlds.

3. Adaptive Learning Systems

AI-powered adaptive learning platforms are set to revolutionize how education is delivered, tailoring content to meet individual needs and learning speeds.

Future Applications:

o Libraries can integrate adaptive platforms that support patrons in mastering skills or exploring new disciplines.

o These systems can provide real-time feedback, helping learners adjust their strategies and improve outcomes.

o   Collaborative adaptive learning tools can connect students and educators across institutions, fostering global educational networks.

4. Blockchain for Digital Credentialing and Knowledge Management

Blockchain technology offers secure and decentralized solutions for managing digital credentials and intellectual property.

Future Applications:

o   Libraries can become repositories for blockchain-verified digital credentials, such as certificates and degrees.

o   Researchers can protect their intellectual property using blockchain-based systems, ensuring transparency and authenticity.

o   Blockchain can support open-access publishing, reducing barriers to academic research dissemination.

5. AI-Augmented Scholarly Communication

AI is transforming scholarly communication, making it more efficient, accessible, and interactive.

Future Applications:

o   Libraries can use AI to automate peer review processes, enhancing the speed and accuracy of academic publishing.

o   AI-powered tools can summarize research papers, making academic knowledge more digestible for wider audiences.

o   Collaborative platforms powered by AI can enable real-time interactions between authors, reviewers, and readers.

6. Real-Time Data Analytics for Research and Learning

As data becomes increasingly central to research and education, real-time analytics powered by AI will play a pivotal role.

Future Applications:

o   Libraries can provide dashboards that offer insights into resource usage, helping institutions optimize their collections.

o   Researchers can analyze live data streams to monitor trends, test hypotheses, and make immediate adjustments to experiments.

o   AI can enhance decision-making in academic institutions by predicting future trends based on historical data.

7. Emotional AI and Sentiment Analysis

Emotional AI, capable of recognizing and responding to human emotions, is emerging as a valuable tool in education and research.

Future Applications:

o   Libraries can use sentiment analysis to gauge user satisfaction and refine services accordingly.

o   AI-driven tools can adapt learning experiences based on a user's emotional engagement, ensuring better outcomes.

o   Emotional AI can support mental health initiatives within educational institutions by identifying and addressing stress indicators in students and staff.

8. Integration of Quantum Computing in Research

Quantum computing promises unparalleled computational power, enabling breakthroughs in complex problem-solving and research.

Future Applications:

o Libraries can offer access to quantum computing platforms, democratizing this advanced technology for researchers and students.

o AI-powered quantum tools can accelerate data analysis in fields like genomics, climate modeling, and materials science.

o Collaboration between libraries and research institutions can lead to the development of quantum-ready educational programs.

9. Sustainable AI for Green Libraries

The rise of sustainable AI practices aligns with global efforts to address climate change and reduce environmental footprints.

Future Applications:

o Libraries can adopt energy-efficient AI tools, minimizing the environmental impact of their digital operations.

o AI can optimize library building management, including lighting, heating, and resource usage, contributing to green initiatives.

o Sustainable AI systems can support research on environmental issues, empowering libraries to contribute to global sustainability goals.

10. AI-Powered Collaboration Platforms

AI is transforming how individuals and institutions collaborate, creating platforms that foster creativity, knowledge-sharing, and problem-solving.

Future Applications:

o Libraries can host AI-driven platforms that connect researchers, educators, and students worldwide.

o Collaborative AI systems can generate shared insights, reducing duplication of effort in research and innovation.

o Libraries can support interdisciplinary projects by using AI to identify and connect complementary expertise across institutions.

In conclusion, the future trends and emerging technologies driven by AI will redefine the role of libraries in education and research. By embracing innovations like knowledge graphs, AR/VR, adaptive learning, and quantum computing, libraries can position themselves as leaders in a rapidly changing digital landscape. These advancements not only enhance the user experience but also ensure libraries remain indispensable in fostering innovation, collaboration, and sustainable development.

Part II: AI Tools and Technologies for Libraries
Chapter 4: Conversational AI and Chatbots

Overview of Chatbots and Virtual Assistants

Conversational AI, embodied in chatbots and virtual assistants, is revolutionizing how libraries interact with their patrons. These AI-driven technologies leverage advancements in natural language processing (NLP), machine learning, and artificial intelligence to provide efficient, personalized, and intuitive communication solutions. By automating interactions and streamlining service delivery, chatbots and virtual assistants enhance the user experience while increasing operational efficiency.

What Are Chatbots and Virtual Assistants?

Chatbots:

o   Chatbots are AI-powered programs designed to simulate human conversations through text or voice.

o   They operate on predefined scripts or advanced machine learning algorithms to answer questions, provide information, and assist users with tasks.

Virtual Assistants:

o   Virtual assistants are more sophisticated AI systems capable of understanding and executing complex commands.

o   They often integrate with multiple platforms and devices to perform tasks like booking resources, managing accounts, or guiding research.

Core Features of Chatbots and Virtual Assistants

1. **Natural Language Understanding (NLU):**

o Enables the AI to comprehend and process user queries in everyday language.

o Allows patrons to interact without needing specialized knowledge of library systems.

2. **Context Awareness**:

o Advanced systems maintain contextual understanding, enabling multi-turn conversations that feel natural and intuitive.

3. **Multilingual Support**:

o AI systems can interact in multiple languages, broadening accessibility to diverse user groups.

4. **Personalization**:

o Machine learning algorithms analyze user preferences to provide tailored responses and recommendations.

5. **Automation**:

o Handles routine tasks like answering FAQs, renewing loans, or providing directions, freeing staff for more complex duties.

Applications in Library Settings

1. **User Support and Assistance**:

o Chatbots answer frequently asked questions about library hours, locations, services, and policies.

o Virtual assistants provide guidance on resource discovery and database navigation.

2. **Resource Management**:

o Assisting users with catalog searches, book reservations, and overdue notices.

o   Offering personalized reading or research recommendations based on borrowing history and preferences.

3. **Event and Program Coordination:**

o   Helping users register for workshops, lectures, or community events hosted by the library.

o   Sending reminders and updates about events.

4. **Research Support:**

o   Providing tools for citation generation, literature searches, and bibliographic management.

o   Connecting users to subject matter experts for in-depth research support.

5. **Accessibility Enhancements:**

o   Supporting users with disabilities by integrating with assistive technologies such as screen readers and voice-to-text tools.

Advantages of Chatbots and Virtual Assistants in Libraries

1. **24/7 Availability:**

o   Ensures access to library services at any time, enhancing convenience for patrons across time zones.

2. **Efficiency:**

o   Reduces wait times by automating responses to common inquiries and routine tasks.

3. **Scalability:**

o   Handles multiple user interactions simultaneously, catering to high-demand periods without additional staff resources.

4. **Cost-Effectiveness**:

o Lowers operational costs by automating repetitive tasks and optimizing resource use.

5. **Improved User Engagement**:

o Provides instant and personalized responses, creating a more engaging and satisfying user experience.

6. **Data Insights**:

o Tracks and analyzes user interactions to identify trends, improve services, and inform decision-making.

Challenges and Considerations

1. **Ethical and Privacy Concerns**:

o Safeguarding user data is critical to maintaining trust and adhering to data protection regulations.

2. **Technical Limitations**:

o Chatbots may struggle with ambiguous queries, requiring periodic updates and human oversight to improve performance.

3. **User Adoption**:

o Some patrons may be hesitant to engage with AI systems, preferring human interaction. Libraries must provide clear guidance and reassurance about the technology.

4. **Initial Implementation Costs**:

o Setting up and maintaining AI systems requires investment in infrastructure, training, and ongoing support.

The Future of Conversational AI in Libraries

As conversational AI technologies continue to evolve, their applications in libraries are expected to expand:

Integration with Smart Devices:

o   AI systems integrated with smartphones, tablets, and smart speakers for seamless access to library services.

Advanced Personalization:

o   Machine learning advancements will allow deeper insights into user behavior, offering hyper-personalized experiences.

Voice Interaction:

o   Improved voice recognition capabilities for hands-free library interactions.

Proactive Engagement:

o   Predictive analytics enabling AI to anticipate user needs and provide proactive assistance.

In conclusion, chatbots and virtual assistants represent a significant leap forward in how libraries interact with patrons, providing scalable, efficient, and personalized services. These tools not only enhance the user experience but also enable libraries to operate more effectively in a digital-first world.

Use Cases in Reference Services

Conversational AI, encompassing chatbots and virtual assistants, is transforming reference services in libraries. Traditionally staffed by human librarians, reference services are critical for guiding patrons through complex queries, resource navigation, and research processes. AI-powered tools now augment these services, providing instant, scalable, and personalized support. By integrating chatbots and virtual assistants, libraries can enhance accessibility, streamline operations, and meet the evolving needs of their users.

1. Answering Frequently Asked Questions (FAQs)

AI chatbots excel at responding to routine inquiries, providing immediate answers to common questions about library operations.

Examples:

o "What are the library's hours of operation?"

o "How do I renew my books online?"

o "Where can I find the archives section?"

Benefits:

o Reduces the workload on library staff by automating repetitive tasks.

o Ensures 24/7 availability for users to access essential information.

2. Assisting with Catalog Searches

Chatbots can guide users in locating books, articles, and other materials within the library's catalog, simplifying the search process.

Examples:

o "Can you help me find books on artificial intelligence?"

o "What resources do you have on Shakespeare's works?"

Capabilities:

o Offering keyword suggestions and refining search queries.

o Linking directly to relevant catalog entries or digital resources.

3. Providing Research Guidance

AI-powered reference tools act as virtual research assistants, offering support for more complex academic and professional inquiries.

Examples:

o "I need resources for a paper on climate change policy."

o "Can you help me find peer-reviewed articles on quantum computing?"

Features:

o Recommending databases and specific journals based on the topic.

o Assisting with citation generation and bibliographic organization.

o Directing users to subject matter experts or specialized collections.

4. Supporting Multilingual Patrons

Conversational AI systems equipped with natural language processing (NLP) can provide reference services in multiple languages, ensuring inclusivity for diverse user groups.

Examples:

o Offering search assistance or answers in the patron's native language.

o Translating complex library resources or instructions.

Benefits:

o Bridges language barriers, enhancing user experience for non-native speakers.

o   Expands library access to global audiences and multicultural communities.

5. Navigating Digital Resources

Virtual assistants help patrons navigate the increasingly complex array of digital resources, including eBooks, databases, and multimedia content.

Examples:

o   "How do I access JSTOR or ProQuest?"

o   "Can you help me download an audiobook?"

Capabilities:

o   Providing step-by-step guidance for accessing digital platforms.

o   Troubleshooting common issues like login errors or download problems.

6. Event and Program Information

Chatbots streamline communication about library events, workshops, and programs, helping users stay informed and engaged.

Examples:

o   "What events are happening this week?"

o   "How can I register for the coding workshop?"

Features:

o   Sending reminders and follow-ups for registered events.

o   Providing real-time updates about schedule changes or cancellations.

7. Facilitating Personalized Recommendations

AI tools analyze user behavior and preferences to provide tailored suggestions for books, articles, or programs.

Examples:

o "Based on my borrowing history, what books do you recommend?"

o "Are there any upcoming events related to data science?"

Benefits:

o Enhances user satisfaction by aligning recommendations with individual interests.

o Promotes library resources and programs effectively.

8. Addressing Accessibility Needs

AI-powered reference services ensure that patrons with disabilities can access library resources and support effectively.

Examples:

o Assisting visually impaired users with voice-guided navigation.

o Supporting text-to-speech and speech-to-text capabilities for accessible interaction.

Impact:

o Reinforces the library's commitment to inclusivity.

o Expands access for all user demographics.

9. Real-Time Analytics for Service Improvement

Chatbots collect data on user interactions, providing libraries with insights into patron needs and behaviors.

Examples:

o   Identifying common reference questions to improve FAQ resources.

o   Analyzing patterns to optimize resource allocation and staffing.

Benefits:

o   Informs decision-making and service enhancements.

o   Helps libraries anticipate future user needs.

10. Bridging Physical and Virtual Services

Conversational AI links in-person and digital reference services, offering a seamless user experience.

Examples:

o   Guiding patrons to physical locations for specific resources or assistance.

o   Transitioning complex inquiries from chatbots to human librarians when needed.

Advantages:

o   Maintains a balance between automated and human-driven support.

o   Ensures comprehensive service coverage for diverse user queries.

In conclusion, conversational AI is revolutionizing reference services in libraries by automating routine tasks, enhancing accessibility, and providing tailored assistance. Chatbots and virtual assistants not only improve operational efficiency but also ensure that users receive timely and effective support for their informational needs. As these tools continue to evolve, their integration into library reference services will be instrumental in shaping the future of library-user interactions.

Best Practices for Chatbot Implementation

Implementing chatbots in libraries requires thoughtful planning and strategic execution to maximize their effectiveness and user satisfaction. As a key tool for enhancing service delivery, chatbots must be designed, integrated, and maintained with a focus on accessibility, efficiency, and ethical considerations. By following best practices, libraries can ensure that chatbots provide seamless support while upholding the institution's mission of inclusivity and trust.

1. Define Clear Objectives

Before implementation, libraries should identify the specific goals and use cases for the chatbot.

Best Practices:

o   Determine whether the chatbot will handle FAQs, catalog searches, research support, or a combination of services.

o   Align the chatbot's capabilities with the library's broader service objectives.

o   Establish measurable performance metrics, such as response accuracy and user satisfaction.

2. Choose the Right Platform and Technology

Selecting the appropriate technology platform is critical for the chatbot's functionality and scalability.

Best Practices:

o   Opt for platforms that support natural language processing (NLP) for intuitive user interactions.

o   Ensure compatibility with existing library systems, such as catalogs, databases, and event management tools.

o   Consider cloud-based solutions for scalability and ease of integration.

3. Prioritize User-Centric Design

The chatbot should be designed with the end user in mind, ensuring ease of use and accessibility.

Best Practices:

o   Use clear and conversational language to engage users effectively.

o   Implement a user-friendly interface, whether text-based or voice-enabled.

o   Offer multilingual support to cater to diverse user demographics.

o   Ensure accessibility for users with disabilities through assistive technologies like text-to-speech or screen reader compatibility.

4. Provide Contextual and Personalized Responses

Chatbots should deliver accurate and relevant answers tailored to individual user needs.

Best Practices:

o   Leverage machine learning to analyze user behavior and preferences for personalized recommendations.

o   Maintain contextual understanding in multi-turn conversations for coherent interactions.

o   Offer options for users to refine or clarify their queries.

5. Maintain Transparency and Ethical Standards

Transparency builds user trust and ensures ethical AI implementation.

Best Practices:

o Clearly disclose that users are interacting with an AI chatbot, not a human.

o Provide an option to escalate complex queries to human librarians.

o Ensure compliance with data privacy regulations, such as GDPR or HIPAA, by securely handling user data.

o Regularly audit the chatbot for algorithmic bias and ensure equitable service delivery.

6. Integrate with Human Support

A chatbot should complement, not replace, human-driven services in the library.

Best Practices:

o Design a seamless handoff process for escalating unresolved queries to library staff.

o Train librarians to work alongside chatbots, using the tool to enhance their interactions.

o Monitor chatbot performance and use insights to inform staff training and resource allocation.

7. Enable Continuous Learning and Improvement

Chatbots must be regularly updated to adapt to changing user needs and emerging technologies.

Best Practices:

o   Use feedback loops to refine responses and expand the chatbot's knowledge base.

o   Implement machine learning models that allow the chatbot to improve its accuracy over time.

o   Regularly review and update the chatbot's content to reflect new library services, policies, and resources.

8. Test Thoroughly Before Deployment

Comprehensive testing ensures that the chatbot functions effectively under various scenarios.

Best Practices:

o   Conduct user acceptance testing (UAT) with a diverse group of library patrons and staff.

o   Simulate high-traffic scenarios to evaluate the chatbot's performance under load.

o   Test interactions in multiple languages and across different devices for compatibility.

9. Monitor Performance and User Feedback

Ongoing monitoring is essential for maintaining high-quality chatbot services.

Best Practices:

o   Track key performance indicators (KPIs), such as response time, accuracy, and user satisfaction.

o   Use analytics to identify common queries and optimize the chatbot's responses.

o Encourage user feedback through surveys and use the insights for iterative improvements.

10. Promote Awareness and Adoption

Ensuring that patrons are aware of and comfortable using the chatbot is crucial for its success.

Best Practices:

o Publicize the chatbot through library websites, social media, and on-site signage.

o Provide tutorials or guides on how to interact with the chatbot effectively.

o Host workshops or events to familiarize users with the chatbot's features and benefits.

11. Plan for Long-Term Sustainability

To maximize the chatbot's impact, libraries should prioritize its long-term maintenance and integration.

Best Practices:

o Allocate resources for ongoing support and updates.

o Build partnerships with technology providers for technical assistance and innovation.

o Regularly assess the chatbot's alignment with library goals and emerging user needs.

In conclusion, implementing chatbots in libraries offers significant benefits, from enhanced user engagement to operational efficiency. However, success depends on thoughtful planning, user-centric design, and continuous improvement. By following these best practices, libraries can ensure that their chatbots not only meet but exceed user expectations, positioning themselves as leaders in innovative and accessible service delivery.

Chapter 5: Intelligent Search and Discovery

AI-Based Cataloging and Classification

AI-based cataloging and classification represent a transformative shift in how libraries organize and present their collections. Traditional cataloging methods, while effective, are often time-intensive and limited in scope, relying heavily on human input to maintain accuracy and consistency. With the advent of artificial intelligence (AI), libraries can now automate and enhance these processes, making their catalogs more dynamic, intuitive, and accessible for users. This shift not only improves operational efficiency but also enables libraries to better meet the evolving needs of their patrons.

1. The Role of AI in Cataloging and Classification

AI-powered systems utilize machine learning, natural language processing (NLP), and semantic analysis to automate and refine cataloging processes. These tools analyze metadata, content, and user behavior to classify and organize resources more effectively.

Key Features:

o   Automated indexing of materials, including books, journals, multimedia, and digital resources.

o   Contextual tagging that captures nuanced themes and subjects beyond basic metadata.

o   Integration with global cataloging standards, such as MARC and Dublin Core, to ensure consistency.

2. Automation of Routine Cataloging Tasks

AI significantly reduces the time and effort required for manual cataloging, enabling librarians to focus on more complex and strategic responsibilities.

Applications:

o Extracting metadata automatically from uploaded files or scanned materials.

o Suggesting subject headings and classification codes based on content analysis.

o Identifying duplicates and inconsistencies in catalog entries.

Benefits:

o Accelerates the cataloging process, especially for large-scale digitization projects.

o Minimizes human error and improves the accuracy of catalog entries.

o Reduces the workload on library staff, freeing resources for other priorities.

3. Enhancing Discovery Through Semantic Classification

Traditional cataloging often struggles to capture the full context and relationships between resources. AI introduces semantic classification, which understands and organizes materials based on meaning rather than keywords.

Features:

o Identifying thematic connections across disciplines and formats.

o Enabling patrons to discover related resources through AI-generated links and suggestions.

o Providing more intuitive search results by considering synonyms, context, and user intent.

Examples:

o A search for "renewable energy" might include results related to solar power, wind turbines, and sustainability policies.

o Historical documents can be grouped by themes, periods, or key figures, enhancing contextual understanding.

4. Real-Time Updates and Dynamic Classification

AI enables catalogs to adapt dynamically to new information and user behaviors, ensuring they remain current and relevant.

Applications:

o Automatically updating classifications as new materials are added.

o Reorganizing resources based on emerging trends or user interactions.

o Highlighting frequently accessed resources or topics of growing interest.

Impact:

o Keeps library collections aligned with current academic, professional, and community needs.

o Encourages discovery of lesser-known resources by surfacing relevant materials in context.

5. Integration of Multimedia and Non-Traditional Resources

Modern libraries host a variety of materials beyond traditional books, including videos, images, datasets, and interactive content. AI facilitates the seamless cataloging and classification of these diverse resources.

Applications:

o Using image recognition to tag visual content with descriptive metadata.

o Applying NLP to index transcripts of audio and video files.

o Cataloging datasets with detailed annotations for research purposes.

Benefits:

o Expands the accessibility of multimedia resources, making them easier to locate and utilize.

o Ensures a unified cataloging approach across all formats.

6. Personalized Discovery Through User Behavior Analysis

AI leverages user interaction data to enhance discovery, tailoring the cataloging and classification system to individual preferences.

Features:

o Analyzing borrowing history and search patterns to recommend relevant resources.

o Customizing classification schemes to reflect user interests or institutional priorities.

o Predicting future resource needs based on trends and historical data.

Impact:

o Improves user satisfaction by aligning discovery experiences with individual goals.

o Encourages deeper engagement with library collections.

7. Collaboration and Interoperability

AI facilitates integration with external systems and platforms, enabling libraries to collaborate more effectively with other institutions.

Applications:

o Sharing metadata and classification schemes across library networks.

o Incorporating linked data to connect local catalogs with global repositories.

o Supporting interoperability with research databases and educational platforms.

Benefits:

o Expands access to external resources and strengthens collaborative research initiatives.

o Reduces duplication of effort by sharing AI-driven cataloging solutions.

8. Challenges and Considerations

While AI-based cataloging and classification offer numerous advantages, libraries must address potential challenges to ensure successful implementation.

Ethical Concerns:

o Ensuring algorithmic fairness and avoiding biases in classification.

o Protecting user privacy when analyzing interaction data.

Technical Limitations:

o   Ensuring compatibility with legacy systems and existing cataloging infrastructure.

o   Managing the cost and complexity of implementing AI solutions.

Human Oversight:

o   Maintaining librarian involvement to validate and refine AI-generated classifications.

o   Balancing automation with the nuanced judgment that human expertise provides.

In conclusion, AI-based cataloging and classification are transforming how libraries organize and present their collections, enhancing discovery and accessibility for users. By automating routine tasks, enabling semantic understanding, and personalizing the discovery process, AI empowers libraries to deliver more efficient and user-focused services. However, successful implementation requires careful planning, ethical considerations, and ongoing collaboration between AI systems and human expertise

Recommendation Systems for Personalized Discovery

Recommendation systems, a cornerstone of AI-powered intelligent search and discovery, are transforming how users interact with library resources. By analyzing user behavior, preferences, and patterns, these systems provide tailored suggestions, ensuring patrons discover materials most relevant to their interests. This personalization not only enhances user satisfaction but also encourages deeper engagement with library collections, positioning libraries as adaptive, user-focused institutions in the digital age.

1. What Are Recommendation Systems?

Recommendation systems are AI-driven tools that predict and suggest items of interest to users based on their preferences, behavior, and contextual data.

Core Technologies:

o **Collaborative Filtering**: Identifies patterns in user interactions (e.g., borrowing history, search queries) to recommend items that similar users have found valuable.

o **Content-Based Filtering**: Analyzes the attributes of materials (e.g., genre, author, keywords) to recommend items similar to those a user has previously accessed.

o **Hybrid Approaches**: Combines collaborative and content-based methods for more robust recommendations.

2. Applications in Libraries

Recommendation systems are instrumental in enhancing the discovery of both physical and digital library resources.

Examples:

o Suggesting books, journals, or multimedia based on borrowing history.

o Recommending scholarly articles related to a user's research topic.

o Highlighting upcoming library events or workshops aligned with user interests.

Use Cases:

o **For Students**: Personalized learning materials and study guides.

o **For Researchers**: Identifying niche articles, datasets, or tools relevant to their field.

o **For General Patrons**: Discovering new books or multimedia content in line with personal preferences.

3. Benefits of Recommendation Systems

Enhanced User Experience:

o Delivers tailored suggestions, reducing the time spent searching for resources.

o Creates a sense of personalization, making users feel understood and valued.

Increased Resource Utilization:

o Encourages the discovery of underutilized resources, ensuring a more balanced use of library collections.

o Promotes awareness of lesser-known but valuable materials.

Streamlined Research and Learning:

o Supports academic and professional pursuits by connecting users to highly relevant resources.

o Helps users stay updated on emerging topics and trends in their areas of interest.

Stronger Engagement:

o Encourages repeat library visits by consistently offering meaningful suggestions.

o Enhances participation in library programs and events through targeted recommendations.

4. Key Features of Library Recommendation Systems

Real-Time Updates:

o   Adjusts recommendations dynamically based on user interactions and new additions to the collection.

Contextual Understanding:

o   Considers the user's current search or query to offer contextually relevant suggestions.

Cross-Platform Integration:

o   Works seamlessly across library websites, mobile apps, and physical kiosks to provide a unified experience.

Multi-Format Recommendations:

o   Suggests resources across formats (e.g., books, eBooks, journals, videos) to meet diverse user needs.

5. Examples of AI-Driven Recommendation Tools

Library Catalog Systems:

o   Incorporating AI to suggest similar items when viewing a resource, such as "Readers who borrowed this also liked..."

Discovery Platforms:

o   Tools like EBSCO Discovery Service and Primo integrate recommendation engines to guide users through digital resources.

Learning Management Systems (LMS):

o   AI-driven systems suggest educational content, assignments, or supplementary materials relevant to a course or curriculum.

6. Challenges and Solutions

Data Privacy Concerns:

o **Challenge**: Collecting user data for personalization may raise privacy issues.

o **Solution**: Implement transparent data policies, anonymize user data, and provide opt-out options.

Bias in Recommendations:

o **Challenge**: Algorithms may reinforce existing biases, limiting diversity in suggested resources.

o **Solution**: Regularly audit and refine algorithms to ensure diverse and equitable recommendations.

Over-Personalization:

o **Challenge**: Excessive tailoring may limit exposure to new or unexpected materials.

o **Solution**: Balance personalized suggestions with exploratory features like "Staff Picks" or "Trending Now."

7. The Future of Recommendation Systems in Libraries

Enhanced AI Algorithms:

o Future systems will incorporate deeper semantic analysis and machine learning to provide even more accurate and intuitive recommendations.

Integration with Emerging Technologies:

o Combining recommendation systems with augmented reality (AR) or virtual reality (VR) to create immersive discovery experiences.

Proactive Discovery:

o   AI could notify users of relevant new acquisitions, upcoming events, or changes in their areas of interest without explicit searches.

Community-Driven Recommendations:

o   Incorporating user reviews, ratings, and shared reading lists into recommendation algorithms for a collaborative discovery experience.

In conclusion, recommendation systems are a transformative tool in AI-powered libraries, enabling personalized discovery and deepening user engagement. By leveraging advanced algorithms, libraries can tailor their offerings to individual needs while promoting the full breadth of their collections. Through careful implementation and ongoing refinement, recommendation systems position libraries as leaders in adaptive, user-focused service delivery.

Natural Language Search and Semantic Search Engines

Natural language search and semantic search engines represent a significant evolution in how users interact with library catalogs and databases. These AI-driven technologies enable more intuitive and precise information retrieval, enhancing the overall user experience. By understanding context, intent, and relationships between concepts, natural language and semantic search engines empower libraries to offer advanced discovery capabilities that align with modern expectations for convenience and accuracy.

1. What Is Natural Language Search?

Natural language search allows users to query databases in everyday language rather than relying on structured keywords or Boolean logic.

Core Features:

o   Processes user input in full sentences or phrases, such as "Find books on the impact of climate change on agriculture."

o   Analyzes syntax, grammar, and context to extract meaningful components of a query.

o   Responds conversationally, mimicking human interactions for a user-friendly experience.

2. What Is Semantic Search?

Semantic search engines go beyond keyword matching to understand the meaning and relationships behind search queries and indexed content.

Core Features:

o   Leverages AI techniques such as natural language processing (NLP) and machine learning.

o   Identifies synonyms, related concepts, and contextual relevance to provide accurate results.

o   Links diverse resources by understanding themes, categories, and ontologies.

3. Benefits of Natural Language and Semantic Search

Improved Accessibility:

o   Reduces the need for technical search knowledge, making library resources accessible to a broader audience.

Context-Aware Results:

o   Offers results that align with the user's intent, even if the exact keywords are not present in the query.

Enhanced Discovery:

o Surfaces related materials that users might not have explicitly searched for, enriching the discovery process.

Faster and More Accurate Results:

o Minimizes trial-and-error searching by delivering precise answers in fewer steps.

Support for Multilingual Queries:

o Facilitates searches in multiple languages, broadening access to global users.

4. Applications in Library Settings

User Queries in Natural Language:

o **Example**: A patron asks, "What are the latest books about artificial intelligence in education?"

o **Result**: The system retrieves books, articles, and multimedia resources based on the query's meaning, not just the keywords.

Contextual Suggestions:

o **Example**: Searching for "Shakespeare's comedies" yields related works, such as critical analyses or multimedia adaptations.

Enhanced Subject Discovery:

o Semantic search links resources with similar themes, enabling cross-disciplinary exploration.

o **Example**: A search for "renewable energy" provides results on solar power, wind energy, and sustainability practices.

Support for Ambiguous Queries:

o   Semantic search clarifies vague terms by considering user history and patterns.

o   **Example**: "Global warming impacts" retrieves a curated set of climate change resources, even if the phrase isn't explicitly used.

5. Key Technologies Powering Natural Language and Semantic Search

Natural Language Processing (NLP):

o   Analyzes and interprets human language for meaningful search interactions.

Knowledge Graphs:

o   Maps relationships between entities and concepts, providing a structured understanding of content.

Machine Learning Algorithms:

o   Continuously improves search accuracy by analyzing user interactions and refining results.

Entity Recognition and Disambiguation:

o   Identifies specific entities (e.g., people, places, topics) in user queries to match relevant content.

6. Integration with Library Systems

Natural language and semantic search engines can be seamlessly integrated into library catalogs, databases, and discovery platforms.

Features:

o   Unified search interfaces that combine physical and digital resources.

o Cross-platform functionality, allowing searches on mobile apps, desktops, or library kiosks.

o Compatibility with existing metadata standards like MARC, Dublin Core, and linked data.

7. Challenges and Considerations

Data Quality:

o **Challenge**: Inaccurate or inconsistent metadata can hinder search engine performance.

o **Solution**: Regularly update and standardize metadata to improve accuracy.

Algorithmic Bias:

o **Challenge**: Search results may inadvertently favor certain perspectives or materials.

o **Solution**: Audit algorithms and diversify training datasets to ensure fairness.

User Training and Adoption:

o **Challenge**: Patrons may need guidance to utilize advanced search features effectively.

o **Solution**: Provide tutorials, demos, and ongoing support to build user confidence.

Cost and Complexity:

o **Challenge**: Implementing and maintaining advanced search engines requires technical and financial resources.

o **Solution**: Partner with technology providers and prioritize scalable solutions.

8. Future Trends in Natural Language and Semantic Search

Voice-Activated Search:

o   Integration of voice assistants for hands-free interaction with library systems.

Multimodal Search Capabilities:

o   Combining text, image, and voice queries for a more versatile discovery process.

Proactive Recommendations:

o   Predictive systems that notify users about relevant new resources based on search history and interests.

Greater Use of AI Knowledge Graphs:

o   Expanding semantic networks to link global library collections, enabling a unified discovery experience.

In conclusion, natural language search and semantic search engines are revolutionizing how patrons discover and access library resources. By making search processes more intuitive, contextual, and accurate, these technologies enhance user engagement and satisfaction while supporting the library's mission to democratize knowledge.

Chapter 6: Digital Preservation and Data Mining

Utilizing AI to Preserve Archives

Digital preservation is a critical aspect of modern library operations, ensuring that historical documents, cultural artifacts, and academic resources remain accessible for future generations. Artificial intelligence (AI) is revolutionizing the field of archival preservation by automating processes, improving accuracy, and enabling deeper insights into preserved materials. By leveraging AI, libraries can efficiently manage, protect, and analyze their archival collections, ensuring their longevity and relevance in the digital age.

1. Challenges in Traditional Archive Preservation

Archiving has long been a labor-intensive process, fraught with challenges such as:

Physical Deterioration: Paper documents, photographs, and other physical media degrade over time.

- **Volume and Complexity**: The growing volume of materials makes manual preservation impractical.

- **Limited Accessibility**: Traditional archives often lack searchable metadata, making discovery and analysis difficult.

- **Resource Constraints**: Preservation requires significant financial, technical, and human resources.

2. The Role of AI in Archival Preservation

AI addresses these challenges by automating and enhancing the preservation process, enabling libraries to digitize, analyze, and maintain archives more effectively.

Key Features:

o   Automation of digitization workflows.

o   Advanced metadata extraction and annotation.

o   AI-driven tools for content restoration and enhancement.

o   Predictive analytics for long-term preservation planning.

3. AI Applications in Archival Preservation

Digitization and Metadata Generation:

o   AI automates the digitization of physical materials, ensuring high-quality digital replicas.

o   Optical Character Recognition (OCR) extracts text from scanned documents, converting them into searchable formats.

o   Machine learning algorithms generate detailed metadata, including keywords, dates, and subject classifications.

o   **Example**: Digitizing historical newspapers and automatically tagging articles with relevant topics for easier discovery.

Restoration and Enhancement:

o   AI restores damaged documents, photographs, and videos by filling in missing details, enhancing clarity, and correcting color degradation.

o   Image recognition algorithms identify and reconstruct faded text or visuals.

o   **Example**: Restoring water-damaged manuscripts using AI to reconstruct illegible portions.

Content Curation and Analysis:

o   Natural language processing (NLP) tools analyze archival content to uncover themes, patterns, and trends.

o   Knowledge graphs map relationships between archival items, linking them contextually for deeper insights.

o **Example**: Using AI to analyze correspondence in a historical collection, identifying key figures, locations, and events.

Preservation Planning and Risk Management:

o Predictive analytics assess the condition of physical archives, identifying materials at risk of deterioration.

o AI models recommend optimal storage conditions, such as temperature and humidity controls.

o **Example**: Monitoring archival materials in real-time to prevent mold growth or chemical degradation.

Enhancing Accessibility:

o AI translates archival content into multiple languages, breaking down linguistic barriers.

o Text-to-speech and speech-to-text tools improve accessibility for visually or hearing-impaired users.

o **Example**: Translating handwritten letters from historical archives into multiple languages for global researchers.

4. Benefits of AI in Archival Preservation

Efficiency:

o Speeds up the digitization and metadata creation processes, reducing reliance on manual labor.

Accuracy:

o Minimizes errors in data extraction and annotation, ensuring consistent and reliable archival records.

Scalability:

o Handles large volumes of materials, enabling libraries to digitize and preserve extensive collections.

Enhanced Discovery:

o   Enriches metadata and links related items, improving resource discoverability for users.

Cost-Effectiveness:

o   Reduces the long-term costs of manual preservation while protecting materials from physical deterioration.

5. Challenges and Considerations

Data Integrity:

o   Ensuring the accuracy and authenticity of AI-processed content is essential for maintaining archival credibility.

Technical Barriers:

o   Implementing AI tools requires expertise, robust infrastructure, and ongoing maintenance.

Ethical Concerns:

o   Protecting sensitive information in archives and addressing algorithmic biases are critical for ethical AI use.

Long-Term Sustainability:

o   Libraries must plan for the preservation of digital archives, ensuring compatibility with future technologies.

6. Future Trends in AI-Powered Preservation

Advanced Restoration Techniques:

o   Emerging AI models will offer greater precision in restoring severely damaged materials.

Immersive Archives:

o   Combining AI with augmented and virtual reality to create interactive archival experiences for users.

Global Collaboration:

o   AI-driven platforms will facilitate international sharing and analysis of archival materials.

Predictive Metadata:

o   AI will anticipate user needs by generating dynamic metadata that evolves with research trends.

In conclusion, utilizing AI to preserve archives represents a transformative opportunity for libraries to safeguard cultural heritage and knowledge for future generations. By automating digitization, enhancing accessibility, and enabling advanced analysis, AI ensures that archives remain relevant and valuable in an increasingly digital world.

Automated Metadata Generation

Automated metadata generation is a game-changing application of artificial intelligence (AI) in the realm of digital preservation and data mining. Metadata serves as the backbone of information organization, enabling effective discovery, retrieval, and management of library collections. Traditionally, creating metadata has been a labor-intensive and time-consuming process. AI-powered tools now automate and enhance this critical task, providing libraries with the means to manage growing collections while improving accuracy and accessibility.

1. The Importance of Metadata in Libraries

Metadata is essential for:

Discovery: Helping users locate resources quickly and efficiently.

Classification: Organizing materials into meaningful categories.

Access: Facilitating seamless navigation across diverse collections.

Preservation: Documenting essential details about resources for long-term management.

2. What Is Automated Metadata Generation?

Automated metadata generation uses AI technologies like natural language processing (NLP), machine learning, and image recognition to extract, analyze, and generate descriptive, structural, and administrative metadata for library resources.

Core Features:

o   Automatically capturing key details such as titles, authors, dates, and keywords.

o   Generating subject headings and classifications based on content analysis.

o   Extracting metadata from multimedia formats, including images, audio, and video.

3. AI Technologies Driving Automated Metadata Generation

Natural Language Processing (NLP):

o   Analyzes text in documents to identify themes, keywords, and categories.

o   Facilitates semantic tagging and contextual understanding.

Machine Learning Algorithms:

o   Learns from existing metadata to improve accuracy and consistency in new entries.

o   Identifies patterns and relationships within data for enhanced categorization.

Optical Character Recognition (OCR):

o   Converts scanned documents into machine-readable text, enabling metadata extraction from physical archives.

Image and Video Recognition:

o   Analyzes visual content to generate descriptive metadata for multimedia resources.

4. Applications in Library Operations

Digitization Projects:

o   Automatically generating metadata for digitized materials such as historical manuscripts, photographs, and maps.

Cataloging New Acquisitions:

o   Streamlining the cataloging process by extracting and populating metadata fields for newly acquired resources.

Enhancing Search and Discovery:

o   Enabling precise and intuitive search results by tagging resources with detailed and accurate metadata.

Integrating Diverse Collections:

o   Harmonizing metadata across disparate collections for unified access and management.

Real-Time Updates:

o   Dynamically updating metadata as resources are modified or new information becomes available.

5. Benefits of Automated Metadata Generation

Efficiency and Scalability:

o   Processes large volumes of materials quickly, significantly reducing the time required for manual cataloging.

Accuracy and Consistency:

o   Minimizes human errors and ensures uniformity in metadata across collections.

Cost-Effectiveness:

o   Reduces reliance on manual labor, optimizing resource allocation.

Enhanced User Experience:

o   Improves discoverability and accessibility by providing detailed and contextually relevant metadata.

Support for Multimedia Resources:

o   Captures metadata for diverse formats, including images, audio, and video, expanding the scope of library offerings.

6. Challenges and Solutions

Data Quality:

o   **Challenge**: Inconsistent or incomplete metadata in legacy collections can affect automation accuracy.

o   **Solution**: Use AI to clean and standardize existing metadata as a preliminary step.

Bias and Fair Representation:

o   **Challenge**: AI systems trained on biased datasets may produce skewed metadata.

o   **Solution**: Regularly audit algorithms and datasets to ensure equitable representation.

Integration with Legacy Systems:

o **Challenge:** Older library systems may not support advanced AI tools.

o **Solution:** Invest in middleware or system upgrades to facilitate integration.

Cost of Implementation:

o **Challenge:** Initial investment in AI tools and infrastructure can be high.

o **Solution:** Prioritize scalable, cloud-based solutions and seek partnerships or grants for funding.

7. Future Trends in Automated Metadata Generation

Context-Aware Metadata:

o AI systems will generate metadata based on the context of user interactions, tailoring results to individual needs.

Semantic Enrichment:

o Enhanced algorithms will link metadata to broader knowledge graphs, enabling richer contextual relationships between resources.

Multilingual Metadata:

o AI will support automated translation of metadata, making collections globally accessible.

Real-Time Metadata Updates:

o AI will dynamically adjust metadata as user behaviors and resource content evolve.

8. Case Study: Automated Metadata in Action

A library digitizing its historical archives used AI-powered OCR to convert scanned manuscripts into searchable text. NLP tools extracted dates, names, and events, generating metadata that linked related documents across the collection. This effort not only improved accessibility but also revealed previously hidden connections within the archives, enriching research opportunities.

In conclusion, automated metadata generation is a transformative tool for libraries, enabling efficient, accurate, and scalable management of diverse collections. By leveraging AI technologies, libraries can enhance discovery, streamline operations, and support long-term preservation efforts.

Text and Data Mining for Enhanced Research Support

Text and data mining (TDM) represents a transformative application of artificial intelligence (AI) in libraries, providing advanced tools for extracting insights from large and complex datasets. By enabling researchers to analyze patterns, trends, and relationships within text and data, TDM enhances research support, opening new avenues for discovery across disciplines. Libraries leveraging TDM not only empower their patrons with cutting-edge tools but also position themselves as integral partners in academic and professional innovation.

1. What Is Text and Data Mining (TDM)?

Text and data mining is the process of using computational techniques to analyze and extract meaningful information from unstructured or structured text and datasets.

Core Processes:

o   Identifying patterns and trends within large corpora of text.

o   Extracting key entities, such as names, dates, and locations.

o   Summarizing content for quick comprehension.

o   Visualizing relationships and connections between data points.

Key Technologies:

o   Natural Language Processing (NLP): Analyzing and understanding human language.

o   Machine Learning: Identifying patterns and generating predictive insights.

o   Data Visualization: Representing findings through charts, graphs, and networks.

2. Applications of TDM in Libraries

Research Discovery and Analysis:

o   Supporting researchers by uncovering trends and correlations in vast bodies of literature or datasets.

o   Enabling meta-analyses by consolidating findings from multiple sources.

o   **Example**: A researcher studying climate change uses TDM to analyze thousands of scientific articles for recurring themes and emerging topics.

Enhancing Access to Digital Archives:

o   Analyzing historical texts, manuscripts, and other archival materials to reveal hidden connections.

o   Supporting digital humanities projects through content mapping and annotation.

o   **Example**: A TDM project uncovers overlooked references to marginalized communities in historical documents.

Systematic Reviews and Literature Summaries:

o Automating the process of reviewing and summarizing academic papers for systematic reviews.

o **Example**: A medical researcher uses TDM to extract key findings from clinical trials on a specific disease.

Cross-Disciplinary Research:

o Bridging gaps between disciplines by identifying shared concepts and methodologies across fields.

o **Example**: Connecting studies on renewable energy in engineering journals with sustainability discussions in social science literature.

Data-Driven Decision Making:

o Helping libraries optimize collections and services by analyzing usage data, patron feedback, and community needs.

o **Example**: TDM reveals underutilized resources, guiding future acquisitions and programming.

3. Benefits of TDM for Research Support

Scalability:

o Processes vast amounts of text and data that would be impractical to analyze manually.

Speed and Efficiency:

o Delivers insights quickly, accelerating the research process.

Deeper Insights:

o Uncovers hidden relationships and patterns that may not be immediately apparent through traditional methods.

Interdisciplinary Collaboration:

o   Facilitates connections between disparate fields, fostering innovative approaches.

Enhanced Accessibility:

o   Makes large and complex datasets more comprehensible through summaries and visualizations.

4. Key Challenges and Considerations

Data Access and Copyright Issues:

o   **Challenge**: Accessing and mining copyrighted materials may raise legal concerns.

o   **Solution**: Use licensed databases or open-access resources to ensure compliance.

Data Quality:

o   **Challenge**: Inconsistent or incomplete datasets can affect the accuracy of findings.

o   **Solution**: Implement data cleaning and standardization protocols before analysis.

Technical Barriers:

o   **Challenge**: Implementing TDM tools requires technical expertise and infrastructure.

o   **Solution**: Partner with technology providers or offer training programs for staff and users.

Ethical Considerations:

o   **Challenge**: Safeguarding sensitive data and maintaining user privacy during mining processes.

o **Solution**: Anonymize datasets and adhere to ethical data usage standards.

5. Tools and Technologies for TDM in Libraries

Open-Source TDM Tools:

o Tools like Python libraries (e.g., NLTK, spaCy) for customizable text analysis.

Commercial Platforms:

o Services like Elsevier's Text Mining Suite or Gale's Digital Scholar Lab provide user-friendly interfaces for TDM.

Visualization Software:

o Tools like Gephi or Tableau for creating visual representations of mined data.

AI-Powered Search Engines:

o Semantic search platforms that incorporate TDM capabilities for enhanced discovery.

6. Future Trends in TDM for Libraries

Real-Time Analysis:

o Developing tools that provide instant insights from live data streams.

Integration with AI Knowledge Graphs:

o Linking mined data to broader knowledge networks for enriched context.

Collaborative TDM Platforms:

o Enabling researchers and librarians to work together on large-scale mining projects.

Increased Interoperability:

o   Creating seamless integration between TDM tools and library management systems.

7. Case Study: TDM in Action

A university library collaborated with researchers to mine digitized newspaper archives for references to public health during the 1918 influenza pandemic. Using NLP and machine learning, the team extracted and analyzed mentions of policies, community responses, and healthcare practices. The findings provided valuable historical context for modern pandemic planning, showcasing the transformative potential of TDM in research.

In conclusion, text and data mining are indispensable tools for enhancing research support in AI-powered libraries. By leveraging TDM, libraries can empower researchers to uncover new insights, accelerate discoveries, and foster interdisciplinary collaboration.

Chapter 7: AI-Enabled Accessibility Tools

Speech-to-Text, Text-to-Speech, and Language Translation

AI-enabled accessibility tools, such as speech-to-text, text-to-speech, and language translation technologies, are transforming how libraries serve diverse user groups. These tools ensure that libraries remain inclusive, breaking down barriers for individuals with disabilities, language limitations, or unique communication needs. By leveraging artificial intelligence (AI), libraries can provide seamless access to resources, foster equitable participation, and support global engagement.

1. Speech-to-Text Technology

Speech-to-text technology converts spoken language into written text in real-time, providing a valuable tool for individuals with hearing impairments, language barriers, or those engaging with audio materials in quiet environments.

Applications in Libraries:

Real-Time Transcription:

- Transcribing library lectures, events, or workshops for live captioning.

- Making audio and video recordings accessible to individuals who prefer or require written text.

- **Example:** Live transcription of a guest speaker's lecture on climate change ensures inclusivity for hearing-impaired attendees.

Voice Command Systems:

- Enabling hands-free catalog searches or resource navigation.

- Supporting patrons with mobility challenges.

- **Example**: A patron uses voice commands to locate books on Renaissance art within the library catalog.

Accessibility in Digital Collections:

- Transcribing audio archives or oral histories to create searchable text databases.

- **Example**: Historical audio interviews are transcribed and tagged for easier discovery and research.

2. Text-to-Speech Technology

Text-to-speech (TTS) tools convert written text into spoken audio, aiding individuals with visual impairments, literacy challenges, or multitasking needs.

Applications in Libraries:

Accessibility for Visually Impaired Users:

- Providing auditory access to digital resources, including eBooks, articles, and websites.

- **Example**: A patron with visual impairments uses a TTS-enabled reader to access journal articles for research.

Multitasking Support:

- Allowing users to listen to resources while performing other activities, enhancing convenience.

- **Example**: Students listen to textbook chapters during commutes using TTS tools.

Support for Literacy Development:

- Assisting patrons with reading difficulties by combining visual and auditory content.

- **Example**: A language learner uses TTS to hear the pronunciation of unfamiliar words in an article.

3. Language Translation Tools

AI-driven language translation tools facilitate multilingual access to library resources, ensuring inclusivity for global and multicultural audiences.

Applications in Libraries:

Multilingual Catalog Searches:

- Enabling users to search for resources in their preferred language.

- **Example**: A patron searches for books on astrophysics in Spanish and receives results with translated metadata.

Document Translation:

- Translating digital resources, such as journal articles, eBooks, or guides, into multiple languages.

- **Example**: An academic paper originally written in French is translated into English for a broader audience.

Real-Time Conversation Support:

- Assisting library staff in communicating with non-native speakers through instant translation.

- **Example**: A librarian uses a language translation app to guide a Mandarin-speaking patron through resource borrowing.

4. Benefits of AI-Enabled Accessibility Tools

Inclusivity:

o Ensures that all patrons, regardless of physical abilities or language proficiencies, can access library resources and services.

Enhanced Engagement:

o Encourages participation by breaking down barriers to communication and resource accessibility.

Global Reach:

o Supports libraries in serving international and multicultural communities effectively.

Operational Efficiency:

o Automates tasks like transcription and translation, freeing staff to focus on higher-value activities.

Improved User Experience:

o Offers personalized and adaptive services that cater to individual needs and preferences.

5. Challenges and Considerations

Accuracy and Reliability:

o **Challenge**: AI tools may produce errors in transcription or translation, particularly with complex or specialized content.

o **Solution**: Combine AI tools with human oversight for critical tasks.

Data Privacy:

o **Challenge**: Ensuring that user data processed by AI tools is secure and compliant with privacy regulations.

o **Solution**: Use encrypted systems and obtain informed consent for data usage.

Integration with Library Systems:

o **Challenge**: Seamlessly incorporating AI tools into existing library workflows and technologies.

o **Solution**: Partner with vendors to ensure compatibility and offer staff training on new tools.

6. Future Trends in AI-Enabled Accessibility Tools

Enhanced Multimodal Interfaces:

o Combining speech-to-text, text-to-speech, and translation in unified systems for a seamless user experience.

Real-Time Translation and Transcription:

o Advancing tools that provide instant, accurate results in live settings.

AI-Driven Personalization:

o Adapting accessibility tools to individual user preferences and learning styles.

Greater Language Coverage:

o Expanding support for less commonly spoken languages and dialects.

7. Case Study: Accessibility in Action

A public library integrated speech-to-text and text-to-speech tools into its digital catalog system, ensuring access for patrons with disabilities. Real-time translation features allowed international users to explore resources in their native languages. The tools increased engagement, with a 30% rise in catalog searches by visually impaired and non-English-speaking patrons within the first year of implementation.

In conclusion, speech-to-text, text-to-speech, and language translation technologies are transforming accessibility in AI-powered libraries. By addressing diverse user needs, these tools foster inclusivity, enhance engagement, and position libraries as leaders in equitable service delivery.

Assistive Technologies for Patrons with Disabilities

AI-powered assistive technologies are revolutionizing how libraries support patrons with disabilities, ensuring equitable access to information, resources, and services. By integrating artificial intelligence (AI) into their operations, libraries can address a wide range of accessibility needs, empowering individuals with visual, auditory, cognitive, and physical disabilities to fully participate in the library experience. These tools demonstrate libraries' commitment to inclusivity and their ability to adapt to diverse user needs in the digital age.

1. Visual Accessibility

AI enhances access for patrons with visual impairments through advanced tools that convert text and images into accessible formats.

Key Technologies and Applications:

Text-to-Speech (TTS):

- Converts written text into spoken audio, enabling visually impaired patrons to access digital and physical resources.

- **Example**: A user listens to an eBook through a TTS-enabled reader.

Screen Readers:

- AI-powered screen readers interpret and vocalize on-screen content, including websites, documents, and applications.

- **Example**: A patron uses a screen reader to navigate the library's online catalog.

Image Recognition:

- Converts visual content, such as images and charts, into descriptive audio or text formats.

- **Example**: An AI tool describes a photograph in an online exhibit for a visually impaired user.

Braille Displays:

- AI translates digital text into Braille for use with refreshable Braille displays.

- **Example**: A library integrates Braille-compatible tools to assist patrons in reading articles.

2. Auditory Accessibility

For patrons with hearing impairments, AI enables access to spoken content through real-time transcription and captioning.

Key Technologies and Applications:

Speech-to-Text:

- Provides real-time transcription of spoken content, such as lectures, events, and videos.

- **Example**: A guest speaker's presentation is transcribed live, enabling hearing-impaired attendees to follow along.

Closed Captioning:

- AI generates captions for recorded videos and live streams, enhancing accessibility for multimedia content.

- **Example**: A library's virtual storytime sessions include automated captions for hearing-impaired participants.

Sign Language Recognition:

- AI tools convert sign language into text or speech, bridging communication gaps between patrons and staff.

- **Example**: A library integrates a sign language interpreter app to assist in patron interactions.

3. Cognitive Accessibility

AI-powered tools support patrons with cognitive disabilities by simplifying content and interfaces for improved usability.

Key Technologies and Applications:

Simplified User Interfaces:

- AI tailors interfaces to be more intuitive, reducing cognitive load for users.

- **Example**: A library website offers an adaptive mode with simplified navigation and larger text options.

Content Summarization:

- AI tools generate concise summaries of lengthy texts, making information more digestible.

- **Example**: A patron with a learning disability uses an AI tool to summarize a research article.

Adaptive Learning Platforms:

- AI systems provide personalized learning resources that align with individual abilities and goals.

- **Example**: A patron with dyslexia uses an AI-powered language learning tool that adapts to their pace.

4. Physical Accessibility

AI assists patrons with mobility impairments by offering tools that enhance navigation and reduce physical barriers.

Key Technologies and Applications:

Voice Command Systems:

- Enables hands-free interaction with library catalogs, kiosks, and devices.

- **Example**: A patron uses voice commands to search for books and reserve materials.

Navigation Assistance:

- AI-powered wayfinding systems provide real-time guidance within library spaces.

- **Example**: A wheelchair user is guided to the accessible entrance and designated seating areas using a navigation app.

Automated Retrieval Systems:

- Robotic tools retrieve books or materials from shelves, reducing physical strain on users.

- **Example**: A patron requests a book via a library app, and an automated system delivers it to the front desk.

5. Benefits of AI-Enabled Assistive Technologies

Inclusivity:

o Ensures that patrons with disabilities can access resources, participate in programs, and engage with library services on equal terms.

Personalization:

o Adapts tools and content to individual needs, providing a customized experience for each user.

Enhanced Engagement:

o Encourages active participation by breaking down barriers to library resources and services.

Operational Efficiency:

o Automates accessibility-related tasks, allowing staff to focus on personalizing support and outreach.

Broad Community Impact:

o Demonstrates the library's commitment to equity and diversity, fostering a welcoming environment for all.

6. Challenges and Solutions

Implementation Costs:

o **Challenge**: High initial costs for AI tools and infrastructure.

o **Solution**: Seek grants, partnerships, or phased implementation to reduce financial burden.

Technical Limitations:

o **Challenge**: Ensuring compatibility with existing systems and hardware.

o **Solution**: Work with vendors to customize solutions and prioritize interoperability.

Training Needs:

o **Challenge**: Staff and patrons may require training to use new tools effectively.

o **Solution**: Offer workshops, tutorials, and ongoing support.

Privacy Concerns:

o **Challenge**: Protecting sensitive data handled by AI systems.

o **Solution**: Implement robust security measures and adhere to data protection regulations.

7. Future Trends in AI-Enabled Assistive Technologies

Advanced Multimodal Interfaces:

o Combining visual, auditory, and tactile features for a seamless accessibility experience.

AI-Powered Wearables:

o Smart glasses or hearing aids that integrate with library systems for real-time assistance.

Immersive Technologies:

o Virtual and augmented reality applications tailored to users with disabilities.

Proactive Assistance:

o AI tools that anticipate user needs and offer support without prompting.

8. Case Study: Empowering Accessibility with AI

A university library implemented AI-powered screen readers, voice command systems, and real-time transcription tools to support its diverse patron base. Within six months, usage metrics showed a 40% increase in resource access by patrons with disabilities, alongside overwhelmingly positive feedback about the enhanced inclusivity of library services.

In conclusion, AI-enabled assistive technologies are essential for creating inclusive library environments that empower patrons with disabilities. By leveraging tools such as speech-to-text, text-to-speech, and navigation aids, libraries can ensure that their services are accessible to all, regardless of physical or cognitive challenges

Inclusive Library Services Through AI

Artificial intelligence (AI) is a transformative force in fostering inclusivity within libraries, ensuring that services, resources, and programs are accessible to all patrons, regardless of physical, cognitive, or linguistic barriers. By integrating AI-enabled accessibility tools, libraries can create equitable environments where every individual can engage with information, participate in community programs, and benefit from library offerings. These tools redefine inclusivity, aligning libraries with their mission to serve diverse communities in the digital era.

1. AI as a Catalyst for Inclusivity

AI supports inclusivity by automating, enhancing, and personalizing library services to accommodate the unique needs of various user groups.

Core Principles:

o **Equitable Access**: Providing resources in formats accessible to everyone, including individuals with disabilities.

o **Personalization**: Tailoring services to the specific preferences and abilities of each patron.

o **Global Reach**: Ensuring language inclusivity to serve multicultural and multilingual communities.

2. Key AI-Enabled Tools for Inclusive Library Services

Speech-to-Text Technology:

o   Converts spoken language into written text for real-time transcription of lectures, events, and multimedia resources.

o   **Use Case**: A hearing-impaired patron accesses live captions for a library-hosted webinar.

Text-to-Speech (TTS) Technology:

o   Converts written text into spoken audio, aiding visually impaired patrons or those with literacy challenges.

o   **Use Case**: A visually impaired user listens to an eBook via a TTS-enabled device.

Language Translation Tools:

o   Breaks language barriers by translating digital resources, catalogs, and communication into multiple languages.

o   **Use Case**: A Spanish-speaking patron browses the library's catalog in their preferred language.

AI-Powered Navigation Systems:

o   Provides real-time guidance within physical library spaces, assisting users with mobility challenges.

o   **Use Case**: A wheelchair user is guided to accessible entrances and resource locations via a mobile app.

Content Simplification Tools:

o   Simplifies complex texts to make information more comprehensible for users with cognitive disabilities.

o   **Use Case**: A patron with a learning disability uses an AI tool to summarize academic papers into digestible content.

3. Inclusive Programming Through AI

AI extends inclusivity beyond resources to encompass library events, workshops, and community programs.

Applications:

Accessible Events:

- Offering live captioning, sign language interpretation, and audio descriptions powered by AI.

- **Example**: A virtual panel discussion includes real-time transcription and translation for global accessibility.

Digital Literacy Support:

- AI tools guide patrons through digital resources, teaching them how to use library systems effectively.

- **Example**: A chatbot assists a senior patron in navigating the library's eBook platform.

Community Engagement:

- Using AI to design programs tailored to the needs of underrepresented groups.

- **Example**: A library analyzes user data to identify gaps in programming for neurodiverse individuals and introduces targeted workshops.

4. Benefits of Inclusive Library Services Through AI

Empowerment of Marginalized Groups:

o AI tools empower individuals with disabilities, non-native speakers, and other underserved populations to access and utilize library services independently.

Enhanced Engagement:

o   Inclusive services encourage broader participation in library programs and resource usage.

Global Accessibility:

o   Language translation and simplified content tools expand the library's reach to international and multicultural audiences.

Improved Community Integration:

o   AI fosters a sense of belonging by addressing diverse needs and ensuring equitable representation in library offerings.

5. Challenges and Solutions in Implementing Inclusive AI

Technical Barriers:

o   **Challenge:** Ensuring seamless integration of AI tools with existing systems.

o   **Solution:** Partner with technology providers and prioritize platforms with strong interoperability.

Cost of Implementation:

o   **Challenge:** High costs may deter adoption, particularly for smaller libraries.

o   **Solution:** Explore grant opportunities and phased implementation strategies.

Bias in AI Algorithms:

o   **Challenge:** Algorithms may reflect biases, affecting the inclusivity of recommendations or services.

o   **Solution:** Regularly audit and refine algorithms to promote fairness and equity.

User Adoption:

o **Challenge**: Patrons may be unfamiliar or uncomfortable with AI technologies.

o **Solution**: Provide training sessions, demonstrations, and ongoing support to build confidence.

6. Future Trends in Inclusive Library Services with AI

Proactive Assistance:

o AI tools that anticipate user needs based on interaction patterns, offering personalized support.

Augmented Reality (AR) Integration:

o Enhancing navigation and resource discovery through AR tools for patrons with disabilities.

AI-Powered Community Analysis:

o Using AI to identify underserved demographics and design inclusive programs.

Universal Design in AI Tools:

o Building AI systems with inclusivity as a core principle, ensuring usability for all patrons.

7. Case Study: AI-Facilitated Inclusivity in Libraries

A city library implemented AI-powered text-to-speech, real-time translation, and navigation tools to enhance accessibility. Within a year, resource usage by visually impaired and non-native-speaking patrons increased by 50%, and attendance at inclusive programs grew by 30%. The library received widespread recognition for fostering an inclusive community space.

In conclusion, AI-enabled accessibility tools are critical for fostering inclusive library services, ensuring equitable access to resources and programs for all patrons. By embracing AI technologies such as speech-to-text, text-to-speech, and language translation, libraries can break down barriers, empower diverse user groups, and reinforce their role as inclusive community hubs.

Chapter 8: AI for Library Operations and Administration

Predictive Analytics for Resource Management

Predictive analytics, powered by artificial intelligence (AI), is revolutionizing resource management in libraries. By analyzing historical data and identifying trends, predictive analytics enables libraries to make informed decisions about resource allocation, collection development, and operational efficiency. This technology ensures that libraries remain responsive to user needs, optimize their expenditures, and proactively adapt to changing demands.

1. What Is Predictive Analytics?

Predictive analytics uses AI-driven algorithms and machine learning to analyze historical data and predict future outcomes. In the library context, it leverages data from circulation records, user behavior, and resource usage to optimize operations.

Core Components:

o **Data Collection**: Aggregating data from various library systems, such as catalogs, user interactions, and facility usage logs.

o **Pattern Recognition**: Identifying trends, such as popular subjects, borrowing habits, or peak facility usage times.

o **Forecasting**: Making data-driven predictions to guide resource planning and decision-making.

2. Applications of Predictive Analytics in Resource Management

Collection Development:

o **Forecasting Demand**: Predicting future trends in user preferences to guide acquisitions.

- o **Optimizing Collections**: Identifying underutilized materials for deaccessioning or promotion.

- o **Example**: Analytics suggest increased demand for digital resources on data science, prompting targeted eBook purchases.

Circulation Management:

- o **Anticipating Borrowing Trends**: Predicting peak borrowing seasons to ensure adequate staffing and resources.

- o **Loan Period Optimization**: Recommending ideal loan durations to balance user satisfaction with resource availability.

- o **Example**: Circulation data forecasts high demand for travel books during summer, enabling proactive adjustments to borrowing policies.

Facility and Space Utilization:

- o **Monitoring Usage Patterns**: Analyzing when and how library spaces are used to optimize layouts and hours of operation.

- o **Planning Expansions**: Predicting growth in user numbers to inform infrastructure investments.

- o **Example**: Predictive analytics reveal that study rooms are consistently overbooked during exam periods, prompting the creation of additional study spaces.

Budget Optimization:

- o **Data-Driven Expenditures**: Allocating budgets effectively based on predicted needs and resource usage.

- o **Cost Avoidance**: Identifying low-impact expenditures and reallocating funds to high-demand areas.

- o **Example**: Analysis shows decreasing demand for printed journals, leading to a shift toward digital subscriptions.

Program and Event Planning:

o **User Engagement Forecasting:** Predicting attendance rates for programs to optimize scheduling and resources.

o **Thematic Relevance:** Identifying trending topics to design programs aligned with user interests.

o **Example:** Forecasted interest in AI topics leads to the development of workshops on machine learning basics.

3. Benefits of Predictive Analytics for Libraries

Improved Decision-Making:

o Enables evidence-based strategies, reducing guesswork and improving outcomes.

Proactive Resource Management:

o Anticipates user needs and adjusts services accordingly, enhancing user satisfaction.

Cost Efficiency:

o Reduces waste by focusing investments on high-demand resources and services.

Enhanced User Experience:

o Ensures timely availability of resources, programs, and facilities that align with user preferences.

Operational Efficiency:

o Streamlines processes, such as staff scheduling and space allocation, based on predictive insights.

4. Challenges and Solutions

Data Quality and Integration:

o **Challenge**: Inconsistent or siloed data can affect the accuracy of predictions.

o **Solution**: Implement robust data integration systems and regularly update datasets for consistency.

Ethical Concerns:

o **Challenge**: Predictive models may unintentionally introduce biases or compromise user privacy.

o **Solution**: Use anonymized data, audit algorithms for fairness, and ensure compliance with data protection regulations.

Technical Expertise:

o **Challenge**: Implementing and maintaining predictive analytics tools require specialized skills.

o **Solution**: Invest in staff training or collaborate with technology partners to bridge expertise gaps.

Adoption Resistance:

o **Challenge**: Staff or users may be hesitant to rely on AI-driven recommendations.

o **Solution**: Provide clear explanations of the benefits and transparency in how predictions are generated.

5. Future Trends in Predictive Analytics for Libraries

Real-Time Analytics:

o Moving from periodic reporting to real-time insights, enabling instantaneous adjustments to services.

Integration with IoT:

o   Incorporating data from Internet of Things (IoT) devices, such as smart shelves or occupancy sensors, to refine predictions.

Advanced Personalization:

o   Using predictive analytics to offer hyper-personalized resource recommendations and services.

Collaborative Forecasting:

o   Sharing predictive models across library networks for regional or global trend analysis.

6. Case Study: Proactive Resource Management Using Predictive Analytics

A large metropolitan library implemented a predictive analytics tool to optimize its collection and services. By analyzing borrowing patterns, the library anticipated a surge in demand for STEM-related resources, leading to a strategic acquisition of eBooks and journals. Simultaneously, space usage data revealed underutilized meeting rooms, prompting a reconfiguration into collaborative workspaces. As a result, circulation increased by 25%, and patron satisfaction scores improved significantly.

In conclusion, predictive analytics is a powerful tool for resource management in AI-powered libraries, enabling data-driven decisions that enhance efficiency, user satisfaction, and operational success. By leveraging historical data and machine learning, libraries can anticipate future needs, allocate resources effectively, and remain proactive in an evolving landscape.

Workflow Automation

Workflow automation, powered by artificial intelligence (AI), is transforming library operations by streamlining repetitive tasks and enhancing efficiency. Automated systems for processes like check-in and check-out have become essential tools, enabling libraries to provide seamless service while optimizing staff resources. By reducing manual effort and minimizing errors, workflow automation improves user experience and supports the broader operational goals of modern libraries.

1. The Role of AI in Workflow Automation

AI integrates into library workflows to handle routine and repetitive tasks, allowing staff to focus on higher-value activities like patron engagement and program development. Automated systems use machine learning, robotics, and data analytics to improve speed, accuracy, and consistency in library operations.

2. Applications of Workflow Automation in Libraries

Automated Check-In/Check-Out Systems:

o **RFID Technology**: Radio Frequency Identification (RFID) tags in library materials enable self-service check-in and check-out processes.

o **AI Integration**: AI optimizes queue management, identifies overdue items, and predicts borrowing trends.

o **Example**: A library's self-service kiosks allow patrons to check out books independently, while an automated system instantly updates the inventory and borrower record.

Inventory Management:

o Automated systems track the location, availability, and condition of materials in real-time.

o AI predicts demand for specific items, optimizing inventory placement and restocking efforts.

o **Example**: An AI-powered system alerts staff to replenish popular titles in high-demand locations.

Automated Fine and Fee Management:

o   AI calculates overdue fines and provides automated notifications for pending payments.

o   Integrates with digital payment platforms for user convenience.

o   **Example**: A patron receives a text message reminder about an overdue book, with a direct link to pay the fine online.

Resource Reservations:

o   Automated workflows handle room reservations, equipment checkouts, and program registrations.

o   AI systems manage scheduling conflicts and suggest alternative options.

o   **Example**: A student uses an online portal to reserve a study room, and the system confirms availability in real-time.

Digital Lending and Returns:

o   Automated workflows support eBook borrowing, ensuring seamless access and instant returns without staff intervention.

o   **Example**: A patron checks out an eBook via a mobile app, and the system automatically returns it after the loan period ends.

Cataloging and Processing New Acquisitions:

o   AI automates metadata generation and classification for newly acquired resources.

o   **Example**: A newly purchased book is scanned, and an AI system assigns subject headings and updates the catalog entry.

3. Benefits of Workflow Automation

Operational Efficiency:

o Reduces manual workload for staff, freeing time for strategic and creative tasks.

o Accelerates processes like check-in, check-out, and inventory management.

Improved User Experience:

o Enables faster service delivery and reduces wait times for patrons.

o Provides self-service options, empowering users to manage their library interactions independently.

Accuracy and Consistency:

o Minimizes human errors in cataloging, inventory tracking, and fine calculations.

Cost-Effectiveness:

o Reduces labor costs associated with repetitive tasks.

o Optimizes resource utilization by identifying and addressing inefficiencies.

Scalability:

o Handles increasing user demands without requiring proportional staff increases.

4. Challenges and Solutions

Implementation Costs:

o **Challenge**: Initial investment in AI-powered systems and infrastructure can be high.

o **Solution**: Seek funding through grants or phased implementation strategies to manage costs.

User Adaptation:

o **Challenge**: Patrons may initially resist self-service systems or find them challenging to use.

o **Solution**: Offer user training sessions, tutorials, and on-site support to build confidence and familiarity.

Technical Maintenance:

o **Challenge**: Automated systems require regular updates and maintenance.

o **Solution**: Partner with reliable vendors for ongoing support and staff training.

Data Security and Privacy:

o **Challenge**: Ensuring the secure handling of user data within automated systems.

o **Solution**: Implement robust encryption and adhere to data protection regulations.

5. Future Trends in Workflow Automation for Libraries

Advanced Robotics:

o Autonomous robots for shelving, retrieval, and inventory audits.

AI-Powered Predictive Analytics:

o Predicting resource demand and user behaviors to preemptively address needs.

Voice-Activated Systems:

o   Enabling patrons to manage check-ins, check-outs, and searches using voice commands.

Seamless Digital Integration:

o   Fully integrated systems that synchronize physical and digital lending workflows.

6. Case Study: A Smart Library in Action

A public library implemented RFID-enabled check-in/check-out kiosks and integrated AI for inventory management. Within six months, the library reported a 40% reduction in staff time spent on routine tasks and a 25% increase in patron satisfaction. Real-time analytics provided insights into borrowing trends, enabling better resource allocation and program development.

In conclusion, workflow automation through AI-powered systems like automated check-in/check-out has become indispensable for modern libraries. These tools enhance operational efficiency, improve user experience, and allow libraries to scale services in line with growing demands.

Enhancing Security and Loss Prevention with AI

Artificial intelligence (AI) is transforming how libraries address security and loss prevention, providing advanced tools to safeguard resources, protect users, and ensure the efficient operation of library facilities. From monitoring physical spaces to preventing material loss, AI-driven systems enhance traditional methods with automation, real-time analytics, and predictive capabilities. By integrating these tools, libraries can maintain a secure environment while fostering an open and welcoming atmosphere.

1. The Role of AI in Library Security and Loss Prevention

AI-powered systems enhance library security by automating surveillance, detecting irregularities, and providing actionable insights. These tools use machine learning, computer vision, and data analytics to improve response times, reduce resource loss, and ensure patron safety.

2. Applications of AI in Security and Loss Prevention

Smart Surveillance Systems:

o   AI-integrated cameras monitor library spaces, identifying suspicious behavior or unauthorized access.

o   Real-time alerts notify staff of potential security breaches or emergencies.

o   **Example**: A computer vision system flags unusual activity near rare book collections, prompting immediate investigation.

RFID and IoT for Material Tracking:

o   Radio Frequency Identification (RFID) tags combined with AI track library materials, preventing unauthorized removals.

o   IoT sensors monitor the movement of items within the library.

o   **Example**: An RFID system alerts staff when a book is taken past the exit without being properly checked out.

Facial Recognition and Access Control:

o   Facial recognition ensures only authorized personnel access restricted areas, such as archives or server rooms.

o   Biometric systems enhance access control for secure zones.

o   **Example**: An AI-driven system grants entry to a staff-only area after verifying identity through facial recognition.

Loss Prevention Analytics:

o   AI analyzes historical data to identify patterns of material loss, such as high-theft items or vulnerable areas.

o   Predictive models recommend preventive measures.

o   **Example**: Analytics reveal that certain journals are frequently unreturned, prompting tighter lending policies.

Visitor Flow Management:

o   AI monitors foot traffic to ensure safe occupancy levels and prevent overcrowding, enhancing security and user experience.

o   **Example**: A real-time occupancy dashboard alerts staff when study areas reach capacity.

Digital Resource Security:

o   AI protects digital collections by monitoring access logs and identifying unusual activity, such as unauthorized downloads.

o   Multi-factor authentication systems secure user accounts.

o   **Example**: An AI system detects excessive downloads from a single account, temporarily suspending access to prevent data breaches.

3. Benefits of AI for Security and Loss Prevention

Proactive Threat Detection:

o   AI identifies potential security threats before they escalate, allowing for swift intervention.

Reduced Material Loss:

o   RFID and IoT systems significantly lower the risk of theft or misplacement of resources.

Enhanced Patron Safety:

o Smart surveillance ensures a secure environment for users and staff.

Operational Efficiency:

o Automated systems reduce the need for manual monitoring, freeing staff for other responsibilities.

Data-Driven Decision-Making:

o Loss prevention analytics inform policies and resource allocation to minimize vulnerabilities.

4. Challenges and Solutions

Privacy Concerns:

o **Challenge**: The use of AI, particularly facial recognition, raises concerns about patron privacy.

o **Solution**: Implement transparent policies, obtain user consent, and anonymize data where possible.

Integration with Existing Systems:

o **Challenge**: Incorporating AI tools into legacy systems may require significant upgrades.

o **Solution**: Opt for modular, scalable solutions that complement current infrastructure.

Cost of Implementation:

o **Challenge**: Advanced AI systems can be expensive to deploy and maintain.

o **Solution**: Seek grants, partnerships, or phased implementations to manage costs.

Technical Expertise:

o **Challenge:** AI systems require specialized knowledge for setup and maintenance.

o **Solution:** Invest in staff training or collaborate with technology providers for ongoing support.

5. Future Trends in AI-Driven Security and Loss Prevention

Predictive Analytics for Risk Assessment:

o AI will anticipate potential security risks based on historical and real-time data.

Behavioral Analysis Systems:

o Advanced AI will recognize patterns of behavior associated with theft or misconduct, triggering preemptive alerts.

Blockchain for Digital Security:

o Blockchain technology will enhance the integrity and traceability of digital resources.

Integration with Smart Facilities:

o AI will sync with smart building technologies for comprehensive security management, including fire safety and emergency protocols.

6. Case Study: AI-Enhanced Security in Libraries

A university library implemented an AI-powered RFID system to monitor physical resources and integrated facial recognition for restricted areas. Within a year, material loss decreased by 35%, and security incidents dropped significantly. Additionally, predictive analytics identified high-risk zones, allowing staff to implement targeted measures, further improving overall security.

In conclusion, AI-powered security and loss prevention tools are critical for modern libraries, offering innovative solutions to protect resources, ensure user safety, and streamline operations. By leveraging technologies such as smart surveillance, RFID tracking, and predictive analytics, libraries can create secure yet accessible environments.

Part III: Step-by-Step Implementation Roadmap
Chapter 9: Laying the Groundwork

Assessing Current Needs and Capabilities

A successful transition to an AI-powered library begins with a thorough assessment of the institution's current needs and capabilities. This foundational step ensures that any AI initiatives are aligned with the library's goals, address user requirements, and build on existing strengths while identifying areas for improvement. By evaluating internal resources, technological readiness, and user expectations, libraries can develop a clear roadmap for AI integration.

1. Understanding Institutional Goals

The first step in assessing needs is to align AI implementation with the library's mission, strategic objectives, and long-term vision.

Questions to Consider:

o   What are the library's primary goals (e.g., enhancing user experience, streamlining operations, expanding digital access)?

o   How can AI technologies support these objectives?

o   What outcomes will define success for this initiative?

Example: A public library aiming to increase accessibility might prioritize AI tools like text-to-speech and language translation.

2. Identifying User Needs

Understanding the expectations and challenges faced by patrons is critical for designing user-centric AI solutions.

Approaches:

o   **Surveys and Focus Groups:** Gather direct feedback from users about their needs and pain points.

- o **Usage Analytics**: Analyze data from library systems to identify trends and gaps in resource usage or service delivery.

- o **Community Engagement**: Involve diverse user groups, including those with disabilities, non-native speakers, and researchers, to ensure inclusivity.

Example: Analytics reveal high demand for STEM resources among students, prompting investment in AI-driven personalized resource recommendations.

3. Evaluating Existing Infrastructure

Assessing the current technological and operational landscape provides insights into the library's readiness for AI integration.

Aspects to Evaluate:

Technological Systems:

- Review existing library management systems, digital platforms, and hardware for compatibility with AI solutions.

- Assess internet connectivity and computing capacity.

- **Example**: A library with outdated cataloging software may need an upgrade before deploying AI-driven search tools.

Staff Skills and Expertise:

- Evaluate the staff's familiarity with AI technologies and identify training needs.

- **Example**: Library staff requires workshops on managing AI tools like chatbots and predictive analytics.

Data Availability and Quality:

- Examine existing data repositories for completeness, accuracy, and structure.

- **Example**: Inconsistent metadata across digital archives may hinder the effectiveness of AI cataloging tools.

Operational Processes:

- Identify repetitive or inefficient workflows that could benefit from automation.

- **Example**: Manual inventory checks could be replaced with AI-powered RFID systems.

4. Benchmarking Against Industry Standards

Comparing the library's current capabilities with industry best practices and peer institutions provides valuable insights.

Approaches:

o Research case studies of successful AI implementations in similar libraries.

o Participate in professional networks and conferences to learn about emerging trends.

Example: A university library explores how peer institutions use AI for digital preservation and integrates similar tools into its workflow.

5. Identifying Gaps and Opportunities

A gap analysis helps libraries pinpoint areas where AI can provide the most value and identify existing strengths to leverage.

Steps:

o List current challenges, such as resource underutilization or inefficiencies in user support.

o Identify specific AI tools or technologies that address these challenges.

o   Prioritize initiatives based on impact, feasibility, and alignment with institutional goals.

Example: A library struggling with high staff workloads may prioritize chatbots for handling routine user inquiries.

6. Building Stakeholder Consensus

Engaging stakeholders early in the process ensures alignment and fosters support for AI initiatives.

Stakeholders to Involve:

o   Library leadership and staff.

o   Patrons, including students, researchers, and community members.

o   IT teams and technology vendors.

Strategies:

o   Present findings from the needs assessment to stakeholders.

o   Highlight potential benefits and address concerns, such as cost or data privacy.

o   Build a collaborative vision for the library's AI transformation.

7. Documenting Findings and Setting Priorities

Summarizing the assessment results in a structured format provides a roadmap for the next steps.

Key Components:

o   A clear overview of identified needs and gaps.

o   An inventory of existing resources and areas requiring improvement.

o   A prioritized list of AI initiatives based on feasibility and impact.

Example: A library's assessment identifies three priorities: implementing AI-driven cataloging, introducing chatbots for user support, and adopting predictive analytics for resource management.

8. Planning for Next Steps

The insights gained during the assessment phase inform the library's strategy for AI implementation, including:

- Selecting suitable AI tools and vendors.

- Allocating budgets and resources.

- Designing pilot programs to test and refine initiatives.

Case Study: Needs Assessment for AI Integration

A public library aiming to enhance accessibility conducted a comprehensive needs assessment. Surveys revealed that patrons with disabilities faced challenges accessing digital resources. The library's analysis identified outdated cataloging software as a key barrier to implementing accessibility tools. Based on these findings, the library prioritized upgrading its cataloging system and deploying AI-powered text-to-speech technology, significantly improving user satisfaction and engagement.

In conclusion, assessing current needs and capabilities is a critical first step in implementing AI-powered solutions in libraries. This process ensures that AI initiatives are strategic, user-focused, and aligned with institutional goals. By systematically evaluating resources, identifying gaps, and engaging stakeholders, libraries can lay a solid foundation for a successful AI transformation.

Building a Vision and Goals for AI Integration

Developing a clear vision and defining specific goals for AI integration are crucial steps in establishing a roadmap for transforming library operations. A well-articulated vision ensures alignment with institutional objectives, provides direction for decision-making, and inspires stakeholder support. Setting measurable goals further translates the vision into actionable initiatives, paving the way for a successful implementation of AI-powered tools and services.

1. Crafting a Vision for AI Integration

A strong vision outlines how AI will shape the library's future, emphasizing its role in enhancing services, improving user experiences, and optimizing operations.

Key Elements of an Effective Vision:

Alignment with Mission:

- The vision should reflect the library's mission and core values, ensuring AI supports its fundamental purpose.

- **Example**: A vision to "leverage AI to democratize access to knowledge and create an inclusive learning environment."

Focus on Transformation:

- Highlight the transformative potential of AI in addressing current challenges and meeting future demands.

- **Example**: "Redefining library services through intelligent automation and personalized user experiences."

Inspiration and Engagement:

- Use language that motivates stakeholders and fosters excitement about the possibilities AI offers.

- **Example**: "Empowering our community with cutting-edge tools to navigate the information landscape of tomorrow."

2. Defining Goals for AI Integration

Goals translate the vision into specific, measurable, achievable, relevant, and time-bound (SMART) objectives. These goals serve as benchmarks for assessing progress and guiding resource allocation.

Categories of Goals:

User-Centric Goals:

o   Enhance accessibility, personalization, and user engagement through AI-powered tools.

o   **Example**: "Implement AI-driven language translation to support multilingual access for all patrons by the end of the fiscal year."

Operational Goals:

o   Streamline workflows, reduce costs, and improve efficiency using automation and predictive analytics.

o   **Example**: "Reduce manual cataloging time by 30% within 12 months through AI-powered metadata generation."

Innovative Goals:

o   Foster innovation by adopting emerging technologies and integrating them into library services.

o   **Example**: "Pilot an AI-driven chatbot for user inquiries, providing 24/7 support within the next six months."

Community Impact Goals:

o   Use AI to address community needs and create inclusive spaces for learning and collaboration.

o   **Example**: "Launch AI-enhanced programs to support digital literacy among underserved populations by next year."

3. Engaging Stakeholders in Vision and Goal Development

Collaborative input ensures the vision and goals resonate with all stakeholders, including staff, patrons, and institutional partners.

Approaches:

Workshops and Brainstorming Sessions:

- Involve stakeholders in discussions about AI opportunities and challenges.

- **Example**: A brainstorming session with staff to identify areas where AI can alleviate workload pressures.

Surveys and Feedback:

- Collect insights from patrons and staff to ensure goals align with their expectations and needs.

- **Example**: Patron surveys reveal a strong demand for AI-driven recommendation systems for resource discovery.

Expert Consultations:

- Engage AI specialists and technology partners to align goals with technological feasibility.

4. Communicating the Vision and Goals

Clear communication is essential for securing buy-in and maintaining momentum throughout the implementation process.

Strategies:

- **Vision Statements**: Publish the library's AI vision in strategic documents, presentations, and marketing materials.

- **Goal Dashboards**: Use visual tools to track progress and share updates with stakeholders.

o **Success Stories**: Highlight early wins from AI initiatives to build enthusiasm and support.

5. Adapting the Vision and Goals Over Time

As the implementation progresses, libraries must remain flexible, adapting their vision and goals to reflect new opportunities, challenges, and user feedback.

Continuous Improvement:

o Regularly review and adjust goals based on outcomes and evolving priorities.

o **Example**: Expanding goals to include AI-driven predictive analytics after successfully implementing chatbots.

6. Case Study: Vision and Goals in Action

A university library developed a vision to "empower research and learning through AI-driven innovation." Goals included deploying an AI-powered search engine to improve resource discovery and implementing predictive analytics to optimize space utilization. Stakeholder engagement ensured the vision addressed both institutional priorities and user needs. The library achieved a 40% increase in catalog search efficiency within a year, demonstrating the effectiveness of its well-defined strategy.

7. Benefits of Building a Vision and Goals for AI Integration

Clarity and Direction:

o Provides a clear framework for decision-making and prioritization.

Stakeholder Alignment:

o Ensures all stakeholders work toward shared objectives.

Measurable Outcomes:

o   Facilitates the evaluation of progress and the demonstration of success.

Increased Engagement:

o   Motivates staff and users by creating a sense of purpose and innovation.

In conclusion, building a compelling vision and defining actionable goals are fundamental steps in successfully integrating AI into library operations. A well-crafted vision aligns AI initiatives with the library's mission, while SMART goals provide measurable benchmarks for success.

Stakeholder Engagement and Buy-In

Stakeholder engagement and buy-in are critical components of successfully implementing AI in libraries. Building trust, addressing concerns, and aligning expectations among stakeholders—library staff, patrons, institutional leaders, and technology partners—ensures that the transformation is collaborative, user-centered, and sustainable. Effective engagement fosters a shared commitment to the library's AI vision, streamlines decision-making, and minimizes resistance to change.

1. Identifying Key Stakeholders

The first step in stakeholder engagement is identifying individuals and groups directly or indirectly affected by AI implementation.

Categories of Stakeholders:

Internal Stakeholders:

▪   Library leadership, staff, and departments responsible for operations, IT, and user services.

External Stakeholders:

- Patrons, including students, researchers, and community members.

- Institutional administrators or board members overseeing library budgets and strategic planning.

- Technology vendors and partners providing AI tools and solutions.

o **Example**: A university library includes faculty, students, and IT staff in discussions about integrating AI into research support services.

2. Building Awareness and Understanding

Educating stakeholders about the potential of AI and its alignment with library goals is essential for generating enthusiasm and support.

Strategies for Awareness:

Workshops and Presentations:

- Conduct sessions to explain the benefits, challenges, and use cases of AI in libraries.

- **Example**: Hosting a workshop on how AI-powered recommendation systems enhance resource discovery.

Case Studies and Success Stories:

- Share examples of successful AI implementations in similar libraries to illustrate impact.

- **Example**: Highlighting a public library's use of AI to automate repetitive tasks and improve service delivery.

Hands-On Demonstrations:

- Allow stakeholders to interact with AI tools, such as chatbots or automated cataloging systems, to experience their potential firsthand.

3. Addressing Concerns and Barriers

Anticipating and addressing stakeholder concerns builds trust and mitigates resistance to AI adoption.

Common Concerns and Responses:

Job Security:

- **Concern**: Staff worry that AI will replace their roles.

- **Response**: Emphasize AI's role in augmenting human work, reducing repetitive tasks, and enabling staff to focus on strategic responsibilities.

Data Privacy:

- **Concern**: Patrons fear that AI tools may compromise their personal information.

- **Response**: Outline robust data protection policies and demonstrate compliance with privacy regulations.

Cost and Complexity:

- **Concern**: Leaders may question the financial and technical feasibility of AI projects.

- **Response**: Present a phased implementation plan with cost-benefit analyses and funding opportunities.

4. Involving Stakeholders in the Planning Process

Collaborative planning fosters ownership and ensures that AI initiatives address diverse perspectives.

Engagement Approaches:

Advisory Committees:

- Form committees with representatives from key stakeholder groups to guide AI planning and implementation.

- **Example:** A committee comprising library staff, patrons, and IT experts evaluates AI tools for user support.

Surveys and Feedback Mechanisms:

- Collect input on user needs, expectations, and concerns through surveys and focus groups.

- **Example:** A survey identifies a strong demand among patrons for AI-driven accessibility tools.

Co-Creation Workshops:

- Engage stakeholders in brainstorming sessions to design AI solutions collaboratively.

5. Establishing Clear Communication Channels

Transparent and continuous communication keeps stakeholders informed and engaged throughout the AI implementation journey.

Communication Strategies:

Regular Updates:

- Share progress reports, milestones, and upcoming plans through newsletters or meetings.

Feedback Loops:

- Encourage ongoing feedback and incorporate suggestions into decision-making processes.

Public Announcements:

- Publicize key developments, such as the launch of new AI tools or pilot programs, to build excitement and awareness.

6. Demonstrating Early Wins

Showcasing quick, tangible benefits builds confidence and strengthens stakeholder commitment.

Examples of Early Wins:

o Deploying a chatbot to handle routine inquiries, reducing staff workload and improving response times.

o Automating metadata generation for newly acquired resources, speeding up cataloging processes.

7. Sustaining Engagement Beyond Implementation

Long-term stakeholder engagement ensures the sustainability and scalability of AI initiatives.

Strategies for Sustained Engagement:

Training and Professional Development:

- Offer ongoing training to staff on AI tools and emerging technologies.

User Empowerment Programs:

- Provide tutorials and resources to help patrons maximize AI-enhanced services.

Evaluation and Feedback:

- Conduct regular assessments to measure the impact of AI solutions and refine them based on stakeholder input.

8. Case Study: Stakeholder Engagement for AI Integration

A city library planning to implement AI for predictive analytics and chatbot services engaged stakeholders through surveys, focus groups, and workshops. Concerns about data privacy were addressed by outlining robust security measures. Early pilot programs demonstrated AI's ability to reduce wait times and streamline resource management. Stakeholders' positive feedback helped secure funding and paved the way for broader adoption.

9. Benefits of Stakeholder Engagement and Buy-In

Increased Support:

o   Builds trust and enthusiasm, minimizing resistance to change.

Informed Decision-Making:

o   Ensures AI initiatives align with user needs and organizational goals.

Collaborative Ownership:

o   Fosters a sense of shared responsibility for the success of AI projects.

Improved Adoption Rates:

o   Encourages stakeholders to embrace new technologies and maximize their benefits.

In conclusion, stakeholder engagement and buy-in are essential for the successful integration of AI in libraries. By involving stakeholders in the planning process, addressing concerns, and demonstrating early wins, libraries can build trust and ensure alignment with user needs and organizational goals.

Chapter 10: Planning and Budgeting

Identifying AI Tools and Vendors

Selecting the right AI tools and vendors is a pivotal step in planning and budgeting for AI integration in libraries. This process involves understanding the library's specific needs, evaluating available technologies, and choosing partners capable of delivering effective, scalable, and user-centric solutions. By carefully assessing options, libraries can ensure a successful implementation while maximizing return on investment (ROI).

1. Aligning AI Tools with Library Needs

The first step is to identify tools that address the library's goals and operational challenges.

Steps to Align Tools with Needs:

Needs Assessment:

- Revisit findings from the groundwork phase to pinpoint areas where AI can provide value (e.g., automated cataloging, user engagement, accessibility).

- **Example:** A library experiencing high demand for multilingual services may prioritize language translation tools.

Goal Prioritization:

- Focus on tools that align with immediate objectives and provide measurable benefits.

- **Example:** Implementing AI-powered chatbots to handle routine user inquiries as a quick-win initiative.

Scalability Considerations:

- Select tools that can evolve with the library's future needs and accommodate increased demand.

2. Researching Available AI Tools

Understanding the landscape of AI tools helps libraries identify options that meet their requirements.

Common Categories of AI Tools for Libraries:

o **User Interaction**: Chatbots, recommendation systems, and virtual assistants.

o **Content Management**: Automated metadata generation and intelligent search engines.

o **Accessibility**: Text-to-speech, speech-to-text, and language translation tools.

o **Operational Efficiency**: Predictive analytics, workflow automation, and RFID tracking systems.

Research Sources:

o Industry reports, professional networks, vendor directories, and case studies of peer institutions.

o **Example**: Reviewing AI tools used by leading academic libraries to identify proven solutions.

3. Evaluating Vendors

Choosing the right vendor is crucial for ensuring successful implementation and ongoing support.

Criteria for Vendor Evaluation:

Experience and Expertise:

- Assess the vendor's track record in providing AI solutions to libraries or similar institutions.

- **Example**: A vendor with a history of deploying AI-driven cataloging systems in public libraries.

Technology Compatibility:

- Ensure the tool integrates seamlessly with existing library systems and infrastructure.

- **Example**: Compatibility with the library's Integrated Library System (ILS).

Scalability and Flexibility:

- Evaluate whether the solution can scale to meet future demands and adapt to emerging needs.

User-Friendliness:

- Consider tools with intuitive interfaces for staff and patrons.

Customer Support and Training:

- Assess the vendor's commitment to providing technical support, updates, and training resources.

Cost and ROI:

- Compare pricing models (e.g., subscription-based, pay-per-use) and evaluate ROI potential.

Security and Compliance:

- Ensure compliance with data privacy regulations and robust security measures to protect patron information.

Questions to Ask Vendors:

o   What is the implementation timeline for this tool?

o   What kind of training and support do you provide?

o   How do you handle data security and user privacy?

4. Conducting Demonstrations and Pilots

Before committing to a vendor, libraries should test tools through demonstrations or pilot programs.

Steps for Effective Pilots:

1.   **Set Clear Objectives**: Define success metrics (e.g., improved response times, reduced manual workloads).

2.   **Engage Stakeholders**: Involve staff and patrons in testing to gather diverse feedback.

3.   **Monitor Performance**: Evaluate the tool's effectiveness, ease of use, and integration capabilities.

Example: Testing an AI chatbot in a small-scale pilot for handling user inquiries before expanding its use across the library.

5. Budgeting for AI Tools and Vendor Services

Understanding the financial implications is crucial for planning and securing funding.

Budget Considerations:

1.   **Initial Costs**: Licensing fees, setup costs, and hardware upgrades.

2.   **Ongoing Costs**: Maintenance, updates, and subscription fees.

3.   **Training and Support**: Costs associated with staff training and vendor-provided support.

Cost-Management Strategies:

o   Seek grants or external funding for technology upgrades.

o   Negotiate flexible pricing models with vendors.

o   Opt for phased implementation to distribute costs over time.

6. Building Vendor Relationships

Establishing a collaborative relationship with vendors ensures a smoother implementation and long-term success.

Best Practices:

o   Maintain open communication to address challenges promptly.

o   Set clear expectations for deliverables, timelines, and support.

o   Regularly review the vendor's performance and seek improvements.

7. Case Study: Selecting AI Tools and Vendors

A public library aiming to implement predictive analytics for resource management conducted a thorough vendor evaluation. After identifying key needs—such as inventory optimization and circulation forecasting—the library shortlisted vendors offering proven AI analytics platforms. A three-month pilot program demonstrated significant improvements in resource allocation, leading to a successful partnership with a vendor that provided scalable solutions and robust customer support.

8. Benefits of a Thoughtful Selection Process

Optimized Investments:

o   Ensures resources are allocated to tools that deliver tangible benefits.

Seamless Integration:

o   Reduces disruptions during implementation by choosing compatible technologies.

Sustained Success:

o   Builds a foundation for long-term collaboration and continuous improvement.

Enhanced Stakeholder Confidence:

o   Demonstrates due diligence in selecting reliable, impactful solutions.

In conclusion, identifying the right AI tools and vendors is a critical step in the planning and budgeting phase of AI-powered library transformation. By aligning tools with needs, evaluating vendors rigorously, and conducting pilot tests, libraries can ensure successful implementation and maximize the benefits of AI technologies.

Creating a Project Timeline and Milestones

A well-structured project timeline with clear milestones is essential for the successful implementation of AI in libraries. It provides a roadmap for tracking progress, managing resources, and aligning stakeholders with project goals. By defining actionable steps, setting realistic deadlines, and incorporating flexibility for adjustments, libraries can navigate the complexities of AI integration effectively and achieve their desired outcomes.

1. Importance of a Project Timeline

A project timeline outlines the sequence of activities required to implement AI solutions, helping libraries:

- **Maintain Focus:** Keeps the project aligned with its vision and objectives.

- **Coordinate Efforts**: Ensures stakeholders understand their roles and responsibilities.

- **Manage Resources**: Allocates time, staff, and budget efficiently.

- **Track Progress**: Provides benchmarks for evaluating milestones and overall success.

2. Key Components of a Project Timeline

Phases of Implementation:

o Break the project into manageable phases, such as assessment, planning, procurement, pilot testing, and full-scale deployment.

o **Example**:

▪ Phase 1: Assess needs and identify tools (Month 1–2).

▪ Phase 2: Select vendors and secure funding (Month 3–4).

▪ Phase 3: Pilot testing and feedback collection (Month 5–6).

▪ Phase 4: Full implementation and staff training (Month 7–9).

Milestones:

o Define measurable checkpoints within each phase to ensure progress.

o **Example**: Completing vendor selection, finishing staff training, or launching a pilot program.

Dependencies:

o Identify tasks that depend on the completion of prior activities to avoid delays.

o **Example**: Pilot testing can only begin after vendor contracts are finalized and tools are installed.

Deadlines:

o   Set realistic completion dates for each phase and milestone.

3. Steps to Create a Comprehensive Project Timeline

Define Goals and Objectives:

o   Revisit the library's AI vision and goals to establish the scope and end goals of the project.

o   **Example**: "Implement an AI chatbot to handle 80% of routine user inquiries by the end of the year."

List Activities and Tasks:

o   Break the project into detailed tasks, including research, procurement, installation, training, and evaluation.

Sequence Tasks:

o   Arrange tasks in logical order, identifying dependencies and parallel activities.

o   **Example**: Staff training may overlap with initial pilot testing to gather real-time feedback.

Estimate Time Requirements:

o   Determine the time needed for each activity, accounting for potential delays.

Assign Responsibilities:

o   Clearly define roles for staff, vendors, and other stakeholders for each task.

Incorporate Review Periods:

o   Include time for stakeholder reviews and adjustments based on feedback.

Use Project Management Tools:

o Leverage tools like Gantt charts, Trello, or Microsoft Project to visualize timelines and track progress.

4. Establishing Milestones

Milestones are critical checkpoints that mark the completion of key activities and ensure the project stays on track.

Characteristics of Effective Milestones:

o **Specific**: Clearly define what constitutes completion.

o **Measurable**: Include quantifiable outcomes to assess progress.

o **Time-Bound**: Assign deadlines to each milestone.

Examples of Milestones:

Finalizing the needs assessment (Month 2).

Selecting an AI vendor and signing contracts (Month 4).

Completing pilot testing and collecting feedback (Month 6).

Training 100% of staff on new tools (Month 8).

Launching full-scale AI implementation (Month 9).

5. Addressing Flexibility and Risks

A timeline must accommodate unforeseen challenges and changes without derailing the project.

Strategies for Flexibility:

1. **Buffer Time**: Include extra time for critical tasks to account for potential delays.

2. **Contingency Plans**: Identify alternative approaches for high-risk activities.

3. **Regular Updates**: Revisit the timeline periodically to adjust for new insights or obstacles.

6. Monitoring and Reporting Progress

Regular monitoring ensures the project remains on schedule and addresses issues proactively.

Monitoring Tools:

o   Use dashboards, progress trackers, and periodic status reports to keep stakeholders informed.

Review Meetings:

o   Schedule regular meetings to discuss progress, challenges, and adjustments to the timeline.

Feedback Integration:

o   Use stakeholder feedback at milestones to refine the subsequent phases of the project.

7. Case Study: AI Implementation Timeline

A university library aimed to deploy AI-driven predictive analytics for resource management. The project timeline included the following milestones:

- Month 1–2: Conduct needs assessment and identify tools.

- Month 3–4: Select vendors and secure funding.

- Month 5–6: Pilot the AI system in one department and collect feedback.

- Month 7–8: Train all staff on the new system.

- Month 9: Launch the system campus-wide.

By adhering to this timeline and incorporating feedback at each milestone, the library successfully implemented the system within nine months, improving resource allocation and user satisfaction.

8. Benefits of a Clear Project Timeline

Improved Organization:

o   Ensures tasks are completed systematically and resources are allocated effectively.

Increased Accountability:

o   Assigning deadlines and responsibilities enhances stakeholder commitment.

Enhanced Communication:

o   Keeps all parties informed and aligned with project goals.

Reduced Delays:

o   Identifying dependencies and potential risks minimizes disruptions.

Measurable Progress:

o   Milestones provide tangible evidence of advancement toward goals.

In conclusion, creating a detailed project timeline with clear milestones is vital for the successful planning and execution of AI-powered library initiatives. A structured timeline helps libraries coordinate efforts, manage risks, and achieve measurable outcomes efficiently.

Cost-Benefit Analysis and Funding Opportunities

A thorough cost-benefit analysis and exploration of funding opportunities are essential components of planning and budgeting for AI integration in libraries. By weighing the financial investment against the anticipated benefits, libraries can make informed decisions that maximize the return on investment (ROI). Additionally, identifying and securing funding sources ensures the sustainability of AI initiatives, enabling libraries to implement transformative technologies without overextending their budgets.

1. Importance of Cost-Benefit Analysis

Cost-benefit analysis evaluates the financial implications of AI projects and determines their feasibility by comparing costs with expected benefits. This process ensures:

Informed Decision-Making: Helps stakeholders understand the financial impact and prioritize initiatives.

- **Resource Optimization**: Guides the allocation of budgets to projects with the highest ROI.

- **Stakeholder Buy-In**: Provides a compelling case for leadership, funders, and other stakeholders to support the initiative.

2. Components of Cost-Benefit Analysis

Costs

Initial Investments:

o Procurement of AI tools, hardware, and software.

o Installation and integration with existing systems.

Ongoing Costs:

o Maintenance, updates, and technical support.

o Staff training and potential hiring of AI specialists.

o Subscription fees for AI services or platforms.

Hidden Costs:

o Downtime during implementation.

o Possible data migration or system upgrades.

Benefits

Operational Efficiency:

o Automation of repetitive tasks reduces staff workload, enabling them to focus on high-value activities.

o **Example**: An AI chatbot reduces human involvement in handling routine inquiries, saving hours of staff time.

Enhanced User Experience:

o Personalized recommendations, 24/7 support, and intuitive interfaces improve patron satisfaction and engagement.

o **Example**: AI-powered search tools help users find resources faster, increasing resource usage.

Cost Savings:

o Reduction in manual labor and operational inefficiencies.

o **Example**: Automated inventory management minimizes resource loss and optimizes stock levels.

Long-Term Value:

o Improved accessibility and inclusion foster greater community engagement.

o Data insights from predictive analytics enhance decision-making.

Measuring ROI

- **Formula**: ROI=Net Benefits (Benefits - Costs)Costs×100ROI = $\frac{\text{Net Benefits (Benefits - Costs)}}{\text{Costs}} \times 100$ ROI=CostsNet Benefits (Benefits - Costs)×100

- Evaluate success through tangible metrics like increased circulation, reduced wait times, and improved user satisfaction scores.

3. Identifying Funding Opportunities

To mitigate financial barriers, libraries can tap into diverse funding sources to support AI initiatives.

Internal Funding

- **Reallocation of Budgets**: Prioritize AI projects by reallocating funds from underperforming services or operational savings.

External Funding

Grants:

o Seek grants from government agencies, nonprofit organizations, or industry partners focused on technology and innovation.

o **Examples**:

▪ Institute of Museum and Library Services (IMLS) grants in the U.S.

▪ European Union Horizon grants for digital transformation.

Philanthropic Support:

o Approach private donors or foundations with a demonstrated interest in education, technology, or community development.

Corporate Sponsorships:

o Partner with technology companies for funding, discounts, or in-kind contributions like software licenses or training.

o **Example**: Collaboration with AI vendors to pilot their tools in exchange for promotional opportunities.

Public-Private Partnerships (PPP):

o Collaborate with businesses to co-develop solutions that benefit both the library and the partner.

Crowdfunding and Community Support

• Engage patrons and community members to support AI initiatives through crowdfunding campaigns or library donation drives.

Collaborative Funding

• Partner with other libraries, institutions, or consortia to pool resources and share costs for large-scale AI projects.

4. Strategies for Securing Funding

Develop a Compelling Proposal:

o Highlight the library's vision, goals, and the expected impact of AI initiatives on users and operations.

o Include a detailed cost-benefit analysis to demonstrate ROI.

Engage Stakeholders Early:

o Build relationships with funders, community leaders, and patrons to garner support.

Leverage Pilot Success Stories:

o   Use outcomes from pilot programs to validate the feasibility and impact of AI initiatives.

Monitor Funding Trends:

o   Stay updated on new grant opportunities and industry developments to identify potential sources.

5. Case Study: Cost-Benefit Analysis and Funding Success

A public library seeking to implement AI-driven accessibility tools conducted a cost-benefit analysis, estimating $50,000 in initial costs and $15,000 in annual maintenance. The anticipated benefits included a 25% increase in resource usage and a 30% reduction in staff workload, yielding a projected ROI of 120% within three years. The library secured a $75,000 grant from a local foundation, covering the initial investment and three years of maintenance, ensuring the project's success without financial strain.

6. Benefits of Effective Cost-Benefit Analysis and Funding Strategies

Financial Feasibility:

o   Ensures projects are sustainable and deliver value within budget constraints.

Increased Stakeholder Confidence:

o   Demonstrates the library's commitment to accountability and effective resource use.

Expanded Opportunities:

o   Access to diverse funding sources enables libraries to pursue ambitious AI initiatives.

Sustainable Growth:

o   Establishes a foundation for ongoing innovation and long-term operational improvements.

In conclusion, conducting a comprehensive cost-benefit analysis and identifying funding opportunities are vital steps in planning and budgeting for AI-powered libraries. These processes ensure financial sustainability, maximize ROI, and empower libraries to implement transformative technologies.

Chapter 11: Designing the Pilot Project

Selecting Focus Areas

Choosing the right focus areas for a pilot project is a pivotal step in implementing AI-powered technologies in libraries. A successful pilot demonstrates the potential benefits of AI, builds stakeholder confidence, and provides valuable insights for scaling initiatives. Focus areas should align with the library's strategic goals, address pressing challenges, and offer measurable outcomes. By starting with targeted, manageable projects, libraries can ensure a smoother transition to broader AI integration.

1. Importance of Selecting Focus Areas

Selecting appropriate focus areas allows libraries to:

- **Demonstrate Impact**: Showcase tangible benefits to users and operations.

- **Manage Risks**: Limit the scope to minimize disruptions and challenges.

- **Generate Insights**: Gather data and feedback to refine larger-scale implementations.

- **Build Momentum**: Create early successes that encourage further investment in AI initiatives.

2. Criteria for Selecting Focus Areas

Alignment with Strategic Goals:

o Focus areas should support the library's mission and long-term vision.

o **Example**: A library aiming to improve user engagement might prioritize an AI chatbot for the reference desk.

Addressing High-Impact Challenges:

o Select areas where AI can provide the most value or resolve pressing issues.

o **Example**: Automated classification to speed up cataloging for a growing collection.

Feasibility:

o Consider the technical, financial, and operational readiness for implementing AI in specific areas.

o **Example**: Implementing an AI-powered chatbot may require minimal system upgrades compared to advanced predictive analytics.

User-Centric Focus:

o Prioritize projects that directly enhance user experience or accessibility.

o **Example**: Text-to-speech tools for visually impaired patrons.

Measurable Outcomes:

o Ensure the focus area provides clear metrics for evaluating success.

o **Example**: Reducing response times for user inquiries by 50% with a reference desk chatbot.

3. Potential Focus Areas for AI Pilot Projects

Reference Desk Chatbot:

Application: Deploy an AI chatbot to handle routine inquiries, such as library hours, book availability, or membership details.

Benefits:

- Reduces staff workload.

- Provides 24/7 support for patrons.

- Enhances user satisfaction through quick responses.

o **Metrics for Success**:

- Number of inquiries handled without staff intervention.

- Average response time.

- User feedback scores.

Automated Classification:

Application: Use AI to classify new acquisitions, generate metadata, and update catalogs.

Benefits:

- Accelerates the cataloging process.

- Improves consistency and accuracy in metadata.

- Frees up staff for other tasks.

o **Metrics for Success**:

- Time saved in cataloging.

- Accuracy of AI-generated classifications compared to manual efforts.

Personalized Recommendations:

Application: Implement an AI-driven recommendation system to suggest books, articles, or programs based on user behavior.

Benefits:

- Increases resource utilization.

- Enhances user engagement.

o **Metrics for Success**:

- Increase in resource usage.

- User satisfaction with recommendations.

Text-to-Speech Tools for Accessibility:

Application: Provide AI-powered text-to-speech capabilities for digital resources.

Benefits:

- Expands access for visually impaired users.

- Promotes inclusivity.

o **Metrics for Success**:

- Number of resources accessed using text-to-speech tools.

- Feedback from users with disabilities.

Predictive Analytics for Resource Management:

Application: Use predictive models to forecast demand for books, space, or digital resources.

Benefits:

- Optimizes inventory and space allocation.

- Improves decision-making.

o **Metrics for Success**:

- Reduction in resource shortages.

- Increase in space utilization efficiency.

4. Steps to Select the Best Focus Area

Conduct a Needs Assessment:

o Revisit the library's current challenges and opportunities identified during groundwork.

Engage Stakeholders:

o Consult with staff, patrons, and institutional leaders to gather input on priorities.

Evaluate Resources:

o Assess the technical, financial, and human resources required for each potential focus area.

Prioritize Based on Impact and Feasibility:

o Rank focus areas based on their potential benefits, alignment with goals, and ease of implementation.

5. Case Study: Selecting a Focus Area for an AI Pilot

A university library faced challenges with resource discovery and frequent staff overload during peak hours. After a needs assessment, the library chose to pilot a reference desk chatbot. This focus area aligned with the library's strategic goal of enhancing user experience while addressing immediate staffing challenges. The chatbot handled 60% of routine inquiries during the pilot phase, reducing staff workload and improving response times by 40%.

6. Benefits of Targeted Focus Areas for Pilot Projects

Early Wins:

o Demonstrates the effectiveness of AI in addressing specific challenges, building confidence among stakeholders.

Reduced Risk:

o Limits the scope of implementation, making it easier to manage and troubleshoot.

Actionable Insights:

o Provides data and feedback to refine the AI solution before full-scale deployment.

Scalability:

o Ensures the chosen solution can be expanded to other areas based on pilot outcomes.

In conclusion, selecting the right focus areas for an AI pilot project is a strategic decision that sets the foundation for successful implementation. By prioritizing high-impact, feasible, and user-centric initiatives, libraries can demonstrate the value of AI technologies and gather critical insights for future scaling.

Defining Success Metrics and KPIs

Establishing clear success metrics and Key Performance Indicators (KPIs) is critical when designing a pilot project for AI-powered libraries. Metrics and KPIs provide measurable benchmarks for evaluating the effectiveness of the pilot, ensuring alignment with the library's goals and justifying further investment. These indicators guide decision-making, highlight areas for improvement, and demonstrate the value of AI solutions to stakeholders.

1. Importance of Defining Success Metrics and KPIs

Measurement of Impact:

o Quantifies the benefits of AI solutions in terms of efficiency, user satisfaction, and cost-effectiveness.

Informed Decision-Making:

o   Provides actionable insights to refine and scale AI initiatives.

Stakeholder Confidence:

o   Demonstrates tangible results, building trust and support for further implementation.

Accountability:

o   Ensures the project remains focused on achieving its objectives.

2. Key Areas to Define Success Metrics and KPIs

User Experience and Engagement

Metrics:

o   Response time for user inquiries.

o   Percentage of queries resolved by AI without human intervention.

o   User satisfaction scores based on surveys or feedback.

Example: A reference desk chatbot reduces average inquiry response time by 50% during the pilot phase.

Operational Efficiency

Metrics:

o   Time saved on repetitive tasks (e.g., cataloging, data entry).

o   Reduction in staff workload.

o   Increase in resource utilization rates.

Example: An automated classification system speeds up cataloging by 30%, allowing staff to focus on strategic activities.

Resource Management

Metrics:

o   Reduction in overdue or lost items through predictive analytics.

o   Optimization of resource allocation based on usage patterns.

Example: Predictive models improve space utilization by 20% in study areas during peak times.

Accessibility and Inclusion

Metrics:

o   Increase in the use of accessibility tools (e.g., text-to-speech, language translation).

o   Feedback from patrons with disabilities or language barriers.

Example: A text-to-speech tool is accessed by 15% of visually impaired patrons within three months of deployment.

Financial ROI

Metrics:

o   Cost savings from automation compared to manual processes.

o   ROI calculated as net benefits relative to project costs.

Example: A pilot project saves $10,000 annually in operational costs, achieving a 150% ROI within the first year.

3. Steps to Define Success Metrics and KPIs

Align Metrics with Goals

•   Identify pilot project objectives and map them to specific, measurable outcomes.

- **Example**: If the goal is to improve user satisfaction, metrics could include user feedback scores and chatbot resolution rates.

Choose SMART KPIs

- Ensure KPIs are Specific, Measurable, Achievable, Relevant, and Time-Bound.

- **Example**: "Resolve 75% of routine user inquiries within 30 seconds using a chatbot during the six-month pilot."

Involve Stakeholders

- Collaborate with staff, patrons, and leadership to select metrics that reflect diverse perspectives and priorities.

Leverage Data Collection Tools

- Use analytics platforms, feedback forms, and system logs to gather relevant data.

Set Baselines

- Establish current performance levels to compare against pilot results.

- **Example**: Measure the average cataloging time manually before deploying an automated system.

4. Examples of Success Metrics and KPIs

For a Chatbot Pilot

Metric: Number of inquiries handled without staff intervention.

KPI: Resolve 80% of routine questions via chatbot within three months.

For Automated Classification

Metric: Average time to catalog new items.

KPI: Reduce cataloging time by 40% compared to manual processes.

For Predictive Analytics

Metric: Improvement in resource availability during peak times.

KPI: Decrease unmet resource requests by 25% during high-demand periods.

For Accessibility Tools

Metric: Adoption rate of accessibility features among target users.

KPI: Achieve a 20% increase in usage of text-to-speech tools within the pilot phase.

5. Monitoring and Evaluating Metrics

Regular Tracking:

o   Use dashboards and reporting tools to monitor progress in real-time.

Periodic Reviews:

o   Schedule check-ins to evaluate performance against KPIs and address any challenges.

Feedback Integration:

o   Incorporate user and staff feedback to refine metrics and improve implementation.

Final Assessment:

o   Conduct a comprehensive review at the end of the pilot to determine overall success and scalability.

6. Case Study: Defining Success Metrics for a Chatbot Pilot

A public library piloted a chatbot to handle routine inquiries, such as library hours and book availability. Success metrics included:

- Resolving 75% of user queries without staff involvement.

- Achieving an average response time of 20 seconds.

- Improving user satisfaction scores from 80% to 90%.

After three months, the chatbot exceeded expectations, resolving 85% of inquiries and reducing staff workload by 30%. These results justified scaling the chatbot to additional services.

7. Benefits of Well-Defined Success Metrics and KPIs

Clarity:

o   Provides a clear framework for evaluating pilot outcomes.

Accountability:

o   Ensures all stakeholders remain focused on achieving measurable results.

Scalability:

o   Identifies strengths and areas for improvement, informing future expansions.

Stakeholder Confidence:

o   Demonstrates the value of AI investments with data-backed evidence.

In conclusion, defining success metrics and KPIs is essential for designing and evaluating AI pilot projects in libraries. Clear, measurable indicators ensure alignment with goals, provide actionable insights, and build a strong case for scaling AI initiatives.

Risk Assessment and Mitigation Strategies

Risk assessment and mitigation are critical components of designing a successful AI pilot project for libraries. Identifying potential risks, evaluating their impact, and implementing strategies to address them

185

ensures smoother execution, minimizes disruptions, and builds confidence among stakeholders. A proactive approach to risk management allows libraries to adapt to challenges, optimize outcomes, and achieve their goals effectively.

1. Importance of Risk Assessment in Pilot Projects

Risk assessment ensures that potential challenges are addressed before they escalate. Benefits include:

1. **Enhanced Preparedness**: Anticipates potential obstacles and provides actionable solutions.

2. **Cost Efficiency**: Prevents costly delays and resource wastage by addressing issues early.

3. **Stakeholder Confidence**: Demonstrates due diligence, fostering trust and support for the project.

4. **Informed Decision-Making**: Enables libraries to balance risks against rewards when scaling initiatives.

2. Common Risks in AI Pilot Projects

Technical Risks

Integration Issues:

o   AI tools may not integrate seamlessly with existing systems.

o   **Example**: Compatibility challenges between an AI chatbot and the library's website.

Performance Gaps:

o   The AI system may fail to meet expectations, such as inaccurate recommendations or slow processing times.

Operational Risks

Staff Resistance:

o   Library staff may resist AI tools due to fears of job displacement or unfamiliarity with technology.

Implementation Delays:

o   Unexpected delays in setup or training can disrupt timelines.

User-Centric Risks

Negative User Experience:

o   Patrons may encounter usability issues or perceive AI tools as impersonal.

Accessibility Challenges:

o   AI solutions may not fully meet the needs of all users, such as those with disabilities.

Financial Risks

Budget Overruns:

o   Costs may exceed estimates due to unforeseen expenses.

Insufficient ROI:

o   The project may not deliver expected benefits, undermining future funding opportunities.

Ethical and Security Risks

Data Privacy Concerns:

o   Improper handling of user data can lead to privacy breaches and reputational damage.

Bias in AI Systems:

o   Algorithms may inadvertently reflect or amplify biases, leading to unfair outcomes.

3. Risk Mitigation Strategies

Technical Risks

Pilot-Scale Testing:

o   Start with a limited scope to identify integration and performance issues.

o   **Example:** Deploy an AI-powered chatbot for FAQs before expanding to complex queries.

Vendor Support:

o   Work closely with vendors to ensure compatibility and address technical challenges.

Regular Monitoring:

o   Use analytics to track AI performance and resolve issues promptly.

Operational Risks

Staff Training and Engagement:

o   Offer comprehensive training and involve staff in planning to build confidence and buy-in.

o   **Example:** Conduct workshops on using AI tools for routine tasks like cataloging.

Phased Implementation:

o   Introduce the project in stages to manage workloads and adjust based on feedback.

User-Centric Risks

User Feedback Mechanisms:

o   Implement channels for users to provide feedback and report issues.

o   **Example**: A feedback form linked to the AI system allows patrons to share their experiences.

Accessibility Audits:

o   Test AI solutions against accessibility standards to ensure inclusivity.

Financial Risks

Detailed Budget Planning:

o   Include contingency funds to cover unexpected costs.

o   **Example**: Allocate 10% of the budget for unforeseen technical adjustments.

ROI Measurement:

o   Define clear metrics to evaluate financial and operational benefits.

Ethical and Security Risks

Data Governance Policies:

o   Establish strict protocols for data collection, storage, and use.

o   **Example**: Use anonymized data to train AI models, ensuring user privacy.

Algorithm Audits:

o   Regularly review AI systems for biases and ensure fairness in outcomes.

4. Steps for Comprehensive Risk Assessment

Identify Risks:

o   Brainstorm potential risks in collaboration with stakeholders, staff, and technology partners.

Analyze Impact and Likelihood:

o   Assess the severity and probability of each risk using a risk matrix.

Prioritize Risks:

o   Focus on high-impact, high-likelihood risks that require immediate attention.

Develop Mitigation Plans:

o   Create action plans to address identified risks.

Monitor and Adjust:

o   Continuously monitor risks and refine strategies based on outcomes.

5. Tools and Frameworks for Risk Management

Risk Matrix:

o   A visual tool to categorize risks by impact and likelihood, guiding prioritization.

Project Management Software:

o   Tools like Trello or Asana to track risks and mitigation actions.

Checklists:

o   Use predefined checklists to ensure all potential risks are considered during planning.

6. Case Study: Risk Mitigation in a Library AI Pilot

A library piloting AI for automated classification identified the following risks:

- **Integration issues**: Collaborated with the vendor to test compatibility with the library's cataloging system.

- **Staff resistance**: Conducted training sessions and highlighted time savings from automation.

- **User dissatisfaction**: Collected feedback on metadata accuracy and refined the AI model accordingly.

By addressing these risks proactively, the library completed the pilot successfully, reducing cataloging time by 30% and earning staff and user support.

7. Benefits of Effective Risk Assessment and Mitigation

Smooth Implementation:

o   Minimizes disruptions and ensures the pilot stays on track.

Increased Stakeholder Trust:

o   Demonstrates preparedness and competence, building confidence in AI initiatives.

Sustainability:

o   Identifies challenges early, paving the way for scalable and long-term success.

Optimized Resources:

o   Reduces waste of time, funds, and staff efforts.

In conclusion, risk assessment and mitigation strategies are integral to the success of AI pilot projects in libraries. By proactively identifying and addressing potential challenges, libraries can ensure smoother implementation, maximize benefits, and build a strong foundation for scaling AI solutions.

Chapter 12: Implementation and Rollout

Technical Setup and Integration with Library Systems

The technical setup and integration of AI tools with existing library systems are crucial phases in the implementation and rollout of AI-powered solutions. This step involves configuring the chosen technologies, ensuring compatibility with current infrastructure, and creating a seamless ecosystem where new and existing systems work in harmony. Proper planning, testing, and stakeholder collaboration during this phase are critical for minimizing disruptions and achieving the desired outcomes.

1. Importance of Technical Setup and Integration

Ensures System Compatibility:

o   Ensures AI tools function smoothly with existing library management systems (LMS), digital catalogs, and databases.

Optimizes Performance:

o   Proper setup maximizes the efficiency and effectiveness of AI technologies.

Minimizes Disruptions:

o   Reduces the risk of technical issues that could impact library operations or user experience.

Enhances Scalability:

o   Lays a foundation for integrating future technologies and scaling AI initiatives.

2. Steps for Technical Setup and Integration

Infrastructure Assessment

Evaluate existing systems, hardware, and software for compatibility with AI tools.

Checklist:

o   Current Library Management System (LMS).

o   Database structure and metadata standards (e.g., MARC, Dublin Core).

o   Network infrastructure and internet bandwidth.

o   Storage and computing capacity for AI tools requiring cloud or on-premise processing.

System Configuration

Configure AI tools based on library needs and technical specifications.

Example: Setting parameters for an AI-powered cataloging tool to align with local classification standards.

3. Integration with Existing Systems

APIs and Middleware:

Use Application Programming Interfaces (APIs) or middleware to connect AI tools with library systems.

Example: Integrating an AI chatbot with the library's catalog search engine for real-time user assistance.

Data Synchronization:

Ensure seamless data flow between systems to maintain consistency and accuracy.

Example: Synchronizing user account data between the LMS and AI tools to personalize recommendations.

4. Security and Compliance

Implement security protocols to protect user data and comply with privacy regulations.

Steps:

o   Encrypt data during transmission and storage.

o   Limit access to sensitive information based on user roles.

o   Conduct regular security audits.

5. Testing and Quality Assurance (QA)

Conduct extensive testing to ensure the integrated system functions as expected.

Key Testing Areas:

o   Functional Testing: Ensures AI tools perform their intended functions accurately.

o   Compatibility Testing: Verifies smooth interaction with existing systems.

o   Stress Testing: Evaluates system performance under peak loads.

o   User Testing: Gathers feedback from staff and patrons to identify usability issues.

6. Backup and Contingency Planning

Develop a contingency plan to address potential failures during implementation.

Example: Setting up backup servers and data recovery protocols to mitigate disruptions.

3. Best Practices for Technical Setup and Integration

Collaborate with Vendors:

o Work closely with technology providers to customize tools and address technical challenges.

o **Example**: Request vendor support for API customization to ensure compatibility with the library's database.

Engage IT Teams:

o Involve the library's IT department to provide expertise in system configuration and troubleshooting.

Conduct Pilot Tests:

o Test the integrated system in a controlled environment before full-scale rollout.

Use Modular Approaches:

o Implement AI tools in phases to reduce complexity and manage risks.

o **Example**: Introduce automated classification in one department before scaling across the entire library.

Document Processes:

o Maintain detailed records of configurations, integrations, and workflows for future reference.

4. Common Challenges and Solutions

Compatibility Issues

Challenge: AI tools may not seamlessly integrate with legacy systems.

Solution: Use middleware to bridge gaps or prioritize upgrades to modern platforms.

2. Data Inconsistencies

Challenge: Discrepancies in metadata formats or database structures can disrupt integration.

Solution: Standardize metadata and clean up data before implementation.

3. System Downtime

Challenge: Integration may temporarily disrupt services.

Solution: Schedule implementation during low-usage periods and provide advance notice to patrons.

4. Security Risks

Challenge: Integration may expose vulnerabilities in data handling.

Solution: Implement robust encryption, access controls, and compliance audits.

5. Case Study: Technical Setup for AI-Powered Cataloging

A university library integrated an AI-driven metadata generation tool with its LMS to streamline cataloging. The technical setup involved:

- Configuring the tool to align with the library's metadata standards.

- Using APIs to synchronize the AI system with the LMS.

- Conducting pilot tests with a subset of newly acquired books.

- Addressing initial challenges, such as inconsistent metadata formats, through data standardization.

The integration reduced cataloging time by 40% and improved metadata accuracy, earning positive feedback from staff.

6. Benefits of Proper Technical Setup and Integration

Enhanced Efficiency:

o   Automates routine tasks, freeing staff for strategic activities.

Improved User Experience:

o   Ensures seamless interactions between patrons and AI tools.

Reduced Errors:

o   Maintains data consistency and accuracy across systems.

Scalability:

o   Establishes a robust infrastructure for future AI integrations.

Operational Continuity:

o   Minimizes disruptions during and after implementation.

In conclusion, the technical setup and integration of AI tools with library systems are critical to the success of AI-powered initiatives. By conducting thorough assessments, collaborating with stakeholders, and following best practices, libraries can create a cohesive and efficient ecosystem that supports their mission and enhances user experiences.

Staff Training and Change Management

Staff training and effective change management are critical for the successful implementation and rollout of AI-powered tools in libraries. These elements ensure that library personnel are equipped with the knowledge and skills needed to use AI systems effectively while fostering a culture of acceptance and collaboration. By addressing potential resistance and providing comprehensive support, libraries can maximize the benefits of AI technologies and sustain long-term operational improvements.

1. Importance of Staff Training and Change Management

Operational Efficiency:

o Equips staff with the expertise to use AI tools, ensuring smooth integration into workflows.

Minimized Resistance:

o Addresses concerns about job displacement or unfamiliarity, fostering acceptance and collaboration.

Enhanced User Experience:

o Empowered staff can better assist patrons, ensuring seamless interactions with AI technologies.

Sustainable Transformation:

o Builds a foundation for continuous improvement and adaptability to future technological advancements.

2. Key Components of Staff Training

Training Needs Assessment

- Identify specific training needs based on staff roles and the AI tools being implemented.

- **Example**: Cataloging staff may need training on AI-powered metadata generation, while reference desk staff focus on chatbot operations.

Training Programs

Customized Workshops:

o Offer tailored sessions that align with staff responsibilities.

o **Example**: A workshop on managing AI-driven predictive analytics for resource allocation.

Hands-On Practice:

o Provide opportunities to use AI tools in simulated scenarios.

o **Example**: Staff practice interacting with a chatbot system as both users and administrators.

Online Resources:

o Use webinars, video tutorials, and documentation for self-paced learning.

Continuous Learning:

o Implement ongoing training programs to address updates or new features in AI tools.

3. Collaboration with Vendors

• Engage vendors to provide expert-led training sessions, user manuals, and technical support.

3. Elements of Effective Change Management

Communication Strategy

• **Transparent Communication**:

o Share the vision, benefits, and impact of AI technologies with staff.

o **Example**: Conduct town hall meetings to discuss how AI will enhance workflows without replacing staff roles.

• **Address Concerns**:

o Provide clear answers to questions about job security, workload changes, and expectations.

Stakeholder Engagement

- Involve staff in the planning and implementation phases to build ownership and trust.

- **Example**: Create a staff advisory group to provide input on AI tool selection and workflows.

Leadership Support

- Ensure library leadership actively supports and champions the change, providing encouragement and resources.

4. Pilot Program Participation

Involve staff in pilot testing to familiarize them with AI tools and gather their feedback for refinement.

5. Recognition and Incentives

- Acknowledge staff contributions and successes during the transition.

- **Example**: Reward staff who excel in adopting and using AI tools with recognition or professional development opportunities.

4. Overcoming Resistance to Change

Resistance to AI adoption can stem from fear of job displacement, unfamiliarity with technology, or skepticism about its benefits.

Strategies to Address Resistance

Empathy and Dialogue:

o Listen to staff concerns and involve them in finding solutions.

Clear Messaging:

o Emphasize that AI is a tool to enhance, not replace, human expertise.

Incremental Implementation:

o   Introduce AI tools gradually, allowing staff time to adapt.

Support Systems:

o   Provide readily available technical support and troubleshooting resources.

5. Monitoring and Feedback

Post-Training Assessments

Evaluate staff understanding and confidence in using AI tools through quizzes or practical tests.

2. Feedback Mechanisms

Collect staff input on training programs and AI tools for continuous improvement.

Example: Use surveys or focus groups to identify additional training needs or usability issues.

3. Performance Metrics

Measure the effectiveness of training and change management through metrics like:

o   Percentage of staff completing training.

o   Staff satisfaction scores.

o   Reduction in errors or inefficiencies post-implementation.

6. Case Study: Staff Training and Change Management in Action

A public library implementing an AI chatbot for reference services launched a comprehensive training and change management program:

Training: Hosted hands-on workshops to teach staff how to operate and troubleshoot the chatbot.

Change Management: Conducted regular meetings to address concerns about job displacement and emphasized AI's role in reducing repetitive tasks.

Outcome: Within three months, 95% of staff reported confidence in using the chatbot, and user satisfaction with inquiry response times improved by 40%.

7. Benefits of Effective Staff Training and Change Management

Increased Adoption:

o   Ensures staff fully embrace AI tools, maximizing their potential benefits.

Improved Morale:

o   Demonstrates the library's commitment to staff development and collaboration.

Enhanced Service Quality:

o   Knowledgeable staff can seamlessly integrate AI tools into user interactions.

Future-Readiness:

o   Prepares staff to adapt to ongoing technological advancements.

In conclusion, staff training and change management are integral to the successful implementation and rollout of AI technologies in libraries. By equipping staff with the necessary skills, fostering collaboration, and addressing resistance, libraries can create an environment that embraces innovation and supports sustained operational improvements.

Patron Awareness and Marketing

Effectively raising patron awareness and marketing new AI-powered services is a critical step in ensuring the success of implementation and rollout in libraries. AI technologies, such as chatbots, personalized recommendations, and automated cataloging systems, bring transformative benefits, but their adoption hinges on user understanding, trust, and engagement. A comprehensive patron awareness and marketing strategy communicates the value of these innovations, encourages utilization, and fosters a sense of inclusion in the library's evolution.

1. Importance of Patron Awareness and Marketing

Encourages Adoption:

o   Clear communication ensures patrons understand the benefits and know how to use new AI services.

Builds Trust:

o   Transparency about how AI works and safeguards privacy fosters confidence among users.

Maximizes ROI:

o   Greater utilization of AI-powered tools justifies the investment and enhances the library's impact.

Promotes Inclusivity:

o   Engaging diverse user groups ensures equitable access to new technologies.

2. Developing an Effective Awareness and Marketing Plan

Understand Patron Needs and Concerns

Conduct surveys, focus groups, or informal feedback sessions to identify:

o Awareness gaps regarding AI technologies.

o User preferences for communication channels.

o Potential concerns, such as data privacy or complexity of use.

Define Key Messages

Communicate the benefits of AI services in clear, user-centric language.

Examples:

o "Find what you need faster with our AI-powered catalog search!"

o "Your personal reading assistant is here—chat with our new AI bot 24/7!"

Choose Appropriate Marketing Channels

Use a mix of traditional and digital platforms to reach diverse patron demographics.

Examples:

o In-library posters and brochures.

o Email newsletters and library website banners.

o Social media campaigns on platforms like Facebook, Instagram, and Twitter.

o Digital screens or kiosks in library spaces.

3. Strategies for Raising Awareness

Demonstrations and Tutorials

Host live or recorded demonstrations showcasing AI tools in action.

Examples:

o   A workshop on using AI-powered search tools for academic research.

o   A video tutorial on interacting with the library's AI chatbot.

Launch Events

Organize special events to introduce AI-powered services, generating excitement and engagement.

Examples:

o   "Meet Your New Library Assistant!" event to unveil a chatbot.

o   A showcase of AI-driven accessibility tools, such as text-to-speech or translation features.

Personalized Outreach

Tailor communications to specific user groups, such as students, researchers, or senior patrons.

Example: Sending targeted emails to students about AI tools for academic success.

4. Building Trust and Transparency

Address Privacy and Security

Clearly explain how patron data is used and protected.

Example: "Your privacy matters to us—our AI tools do not store personal information beyond your session."

Share Success Stories

Highlight examples of patrons benefiting from AI tools.

Example: "John used our AI-powered recommendation system to find books that helped him ace his exam!"

5. Measuring Impact and Adjusting Marketing Efforts

Track Utilization Metrics

Measure adoption rates of AI tools, such as the number of chatbot interactions or catalog searches.

Collect Patron Feedback

Use surveys, suggestion boxes, or digital forms to gather input on user experiences.

Example: "Tell us how our new AI chatbot is working for you— your feedback helps us improve!"

Iterate Campaigns

Refine messaging and outreach strategies based on user responses and engagement levels.

6. Case Study: Marketing AI Services in a Public Library

A public library introduced an AI-powered chatbot for handling patron inquiries. To raise awareness:

Pre-Launch:

o   Conducted a survey to gauge patron interest in virtual assistance.

o   Created posters and social media posts teasing the launch.

Launch Phase:

o   Hosted a live demonstration event attended by over 100 patrons.

o   Distributed brochures explaining the chatbot's capabilities and privacy safeguards.

Post-Launch:

o   Monitored chatbot usage, noting a 50% increase in after-hours inquiries resolved.

o Collected feedback through a digital survey, which highlighted areas for improvement.

7. Benefits of an Effective Patron Awareness and Marketing Strategy

Increased Engagement:

o More patrons adopt and benefit from AI-powered services.

Improved User Experience:

o Patrons feel supported and confident in using new tools.

Stronger Community Connection:

o Effective marketing positions the library as an innovative and inclusive hub.

Sustained Adoption:

o Continuous outreach and feedback loops ensure long-term success.

In conclusion, patron awareness and marketing are vital for the successful rollout of AI-powered library services. By understanding user needs, crafting clear messages, and leveraging diverse communication channels, libraries can ensure patrons embrace and benefit from innovative technologies.

Chapter 13: Evaluation and Iteration

Measuring Performance and Gathering Feedback

Measuring performance and gathering feedback are essential steps in evaluating the success of AI-powered initiatives in libraries. These processes provide critical insights into how well AI tools are meeting their objectives, highlight areas for improvement, and guide iterative enhancements. By leveraging both quantitative metrics and qualitative input, libraries can ensure that their AI systems deliver value, remain user-centric, and adapt to evolving needs.

1. Importance of Measuring Performance and Feedback Collection

Ensures Accountability:

o   Validates that AI implementations align with defined goals and deliver expected outcomes.

Enhances User Satisfaction:

o   Incorporates user insights to refine AI tools and improve user experiences.

Supports Continuous Improvement:

o   Identifies gaps and opportunities for optimization in AI functionalities.

Demonstrates ROI:

o   Provides tangible evidence of benefits, justifying investments and securing stakeholder support.

2. Key Metrics for Measuring Performance

Operational Efficiency

Metrics:

o Reduction in time spent on manual tasks.

o Increase in throughput for processes like cataloging or resource discovery.

o System uptime and reliability.

Example: An AI-powered cataloging tool reduces cataloging time by 40% compared to manual methods.

User Engagement and Satisfaction

Metrics:

o Adoption rates of AI tools (e.g., chatbot usage, personalized recommendations).

o Average response time for user inquiries.

o User satisfaction scores collected via surveys.

Example: A chatbot resolves 80% of routine inquiries within 30 seconds, achieving a 90% user satisfaction score.

Accessibility and Inclusivity

Metrics:

o Utilization rates of accessibility features (e.g., text-to-speech tools, language translation).

o Feedback from patrons with disabilities or language barriers.

Example: Usage of text-to-speech tools increases by 25% within the first quarter of implementation.

Financial ROI

Metrics:

o Cost savings from automation.

o   Increase in resource utilization or patron retention rates.

Example: Automating routine inquiries saves $15,000 annually in staff time.

3. Methods for Gathering Feedback

Patron Feedback

Surveys and Questionnaires:

o   Collect insights on user experiences, challenges, and satisfaction with AI tools.

o   **Example**: "How satisfied are you with the chatbot's ability to resolve your inquiry?"

Focus Groups:

o   Engage diverse user groups to discuss their experiences and expectations.

Feedback Forms:

o   Include feedback options within AI tools, such as a thumbs-up/down feature for chatbot responses.

Staff Feedback

Workshops and Discussions:

o   Host sessions for staff to share their observations and suggestions.

o   **Example**: A monthly meeting to review the effectiveness of AI-powered classification systems.

Anonymous Feedback Channels:

o   Encourage honest input on challenges and improvement areas.

System Logs and Analytics

Analyze data generated by AI tools, such as:

o   Chatbot interaction logs to identify common queries or unresolved issues.

o   Search engine analytics to assess the effectiveness of recommendations.

Third-Party Reviews

Collaborate with external experts to evaluate AI tool performance and usability.

4. Iterative Enhancements Based on Feedback

Prioritize Issues

Categorize feedback into high-priority (critical issues) and low-priority (nice-to-have improvements).

Collaborate with Vendors

Share findings with AI vendors to refine algorithms, update features, or address bugs.

Conduct Incremental Updates

Roll out updates in phases, allowing time for testing and feedback collection.

Re-Evaluate Metrics

Monitor the impact of changes on performance metrics and user satisfaction.

5. Tools for Measuring and Gathering Feedback

Survey Platforms:

Tools like Google Forms, SurveyMonkey, or Typeform for collecting user input.

Analytics Dashboards:

Platforms like Google Analytics, Power BI, or in-built AI tool dashboards for performance monitoring.

Feedback Management Systems:

Software like Zendesk or UserVoice to centralize and analyze feedback.

6. Case Study: Performance Measurement for a Chatbot Implementation

A public library implemented an AI chatbot to handle routine inquiries. During the evaluation phase:

Metrics Measured:

o   Number of queries resolved autonomously (75% of total inquiries).

o   Average response time (20 seconds).

o   User satisfaction (88% positive).

Feedback Collection:

o   Surveys revealed users wanted more detailed responses for complex queries.

o   Chatbot logs identified frequent inquiries about library events, prompting the addition of an events FAQ section.

Outcome: Enhancements led to a 15% increase in user satisfaction and reduced unresolved queries by 10%.

7. Benefits of Measuring Performance and Gathering Feedback

Improved AI Effectiveness:

Continuous refinement ensures tools meet user needs and expectations.

Increased User Trust:

Addressing feedback demonstrates a commitment to user-centric services.

Operational Insights:

Performance data informs decisions about scaling or expanding AI initiatives.

Justification for Expansion:

Positive results support the case for additional investments in AI technologies.

In conclusion, measuring performance and gathering feedback are essential for evaluating the impact of AI-powered initiatives in libraries. By combining data-driven metrics with qualitative insights, libraries can refine their tools, enhance user experiences, and ensure long-term success.

Ongoing Maintenance and Support

Ongoing maintenance and support are vital to sustaining the success and functionality of AI-powered solutions in libraries. After implementation, regular updates, monitoring, and user support ensure that AI tools continue to meet user needs, adapt to evolving requirements, and operate efficiently. A proactive approach to maintenance and support enhances system reliability, builds user trust, and maximizes the return on investment (ROI).

1. Importance of Ongoing Maintenance and Support

Ensures Longevity:

Keeps AI tools functional and relevant over time by addressing technical and operational challenges.

Enhances Performance:

Regular updates optimize algorithms and improve user experiences.

Builds Trust and Satisfaction:

Demonstrating commitment to high-quality services fosters user confidence.

Adapts to Changing Needs:

Allows AI tools to evolve in response to feedback, new technologies, and emerging trends.

2. Key Components of Ongoing Maintenance

System Monitoring

Real-Time Performance Tracking:

o   Monitor system performance to detect and resolve issues promptly.

o   **Example:** Use analytics dashboards to track chatbot uptime and response times.

Error Logging and Resolution:

Maintain logs to identify patterns in errors or failures for proactive troubleshooting.

Software Updates

Feature Enhancements:

o   Regularly update AI tools with new functionalities based on user needs and feedback.

o   **Example**: Adding advanced search filters to an AI-powered cataloging system.

Bug Fixes:

Address technical glitches to ensure seamless operation.

Security Patches:

Implement updates to protect against cybersecurity threats and comply with data privacy regulations.

3. Data Maintenance

Metadata Accuracy:

Regularly audit and update metadata to maintain the quality of AI-powered search and recommendation systems.

Data Cleansing:

Remove outdated or incorrect data to improve AI performance.

Algorithm Retraining:

Retrain AI models with updated data to enhance accuracy and relevance.

User Support

Help Desks and Troubleshooting:

Provide accessible support for users encountering issues with AI tools.

FAQs and Tutorials:

Develop resources to guide users in navigating new features and functionalities.

Feedback Mechanisms:

Continuously collect user input to identify areas for improvement.

Key Strategies for Effective Maintenance and Support

Establish Maintenance Schedules

Plan routine checks and updates to prevent disruptions.

Example: Schedule monthly performance audits and quarterly software updates.

Collaborate with Vendors

Leverage vendor expertise for technical support, updates, and troubleshooting.

Example: Partner with the AI tool provider for annual system evaluations.

Build an In-House Support Team

Train library staff to manage routine maintenance tasks and assist users effectively.

Automate Monitoring Processes

Use AI-powered monitoring tools to detect anomalies and alert administrators in real time.

5. Create a User-Centric Feedback Loop

Actively engage with users to understand their needs and address their concerns.

Example: Regularly survey patrons to identify issues with AI tools and prioritize improvements.

4. Challenges in Ongoing Maintenance and Support

Resource Constraints

Challenge: Limited budgets and staff expertise may hinder effective maintenance.

Solution: Optimize resources by automating tasks and partnering with vendors for critical support.

Rapid Technological Changes

Challenge: Keeping pace with advancements in AI technology.

Solution: Invest in continuous staff training and stay updated on industry trends.

Data Privacy and Security

Challenge: Ensuring compliance with evolving regulations.

Solution: Regularly update security protocols and conduct audits.

User Adaptation

Challenge: Users may struggle with new or updated functionalities.

Solution: Provide ongoing education and accessible help resources.

5. Measuring the Effectiveness of Maintenance and Support

System Reliability Metrics:

Uptime percentages and frequency of disruptions.

User Satisfaction Scores:

Feedback from surveys and support interactions.

Resolution Time:

Average time taken to address technical issues.

Adoption Rates:

Continued usage of AI tools over time.

6. Case Study: Maintaining an AI-Powered Chatbot

A university library implemented an AI chatbot for user inquiries. To ensure ongoing success:

Monitoring: Used analytics to track query resolution rates and identify performance bottlenecks.

Updates: Incorporated user feedback to improve the chatbot's ability to handle complex queries.

Support: Provided a dedicated help desk for users requiring assistance with the chatbot.

Outcome: Chatbot adoption increased by 30% over the first year, with user satisfaction scores rising by 20%.

7. Benefits of Ongoing Maintenance and Support

Consistent Service Quality:

Ensures AI tools operate at peak performance.

Enhanced User Experience:

Regular updates address user needs and improve functionality.

Long-Term ROI:

Prolongs the value and lifespan of AI investments.

Future-Readiness:

Positions the library to adopt emerging technologies seamlessly.

In conclusion, ongoing maintenance and support are critical for the sustained success of AI-powered libraries. By implementing robust monitoring, providing user-centric support, and staying proactive with updates, libraries can ensure their AI tools remain effective and impactful.

Scaling Up and Continuous Improvement

Scaling up and continuous improvement are integral to the long-term success of AI-powered initiatives in libraries. After the initial implementation and evaluation phases, expanding the scope of AI tools and refining their functionalities based on user feedback and performance data ensures sustained impact and adaptability. These steps not only enhance the value of AI investments but also position libraries as dynamic institutions capable of meeting evolving user needs.

1. Importance of Scaling Up and Continuous Improvement

Maximizing ROI:

Expanding AI applications across more services ensures libraries fully leverage their initial investment.

Enhancing Service Quality:

Iterative improvements address gaps, optimize performance, and provide a better user experience.

Meeting Evolving Needs:

Continuous updates and scaling allow libraries to adapt to changing user expectations and technological advancements.

Promoting Innovation:

Scaling AI across services fosters a culture of innovation within the library.

2. Steps for Scaling Up AI Initiatives

Identify Expansion Opportunities

Evaluate which library services can benefit from AI based on pilot project outcomes and user feedback.

Examples:

o   Scaling chatbots to handle more complex queries.

o   Expanding automated cataloging to include multimedia resources.

2. Prioritize Based on Impact and Feasibility

Use criteria such as resource availability, user demand, and technical readiness to determine the order of expansion.

Example: Implement predictive analytics for resource management before introducing virtual reality (VR)-based search tools.

3. Create a Phased Rollout Plan

Implement new AI applications in stages to manage resources and mitigate risks.

Example: Roll out AI-driven accessibility tools for eBooks first, followed by physical materials.

4. Engage Stakeholders

Involve staff and patrons in decision-making and testing to ensure alignment with user needs.

Example: Host focus groups to gather input on expanding AI-powered recommendation systems.

5. Allocate Resources

Secure funding, staff, and technical infrastructure required for scaling.

Explore partnerships, grants, and vendor support to reduce financial constraints.

3. Continuous Improvement Strategies

Leverage Data Analytics

Regularly analyze performance metrics to identify areas for refinement.

Example: Use chatbot interaction logs to enhance its ability to handle frequently asked complex questions.

Incorporate User Feedback

Actively collect and act on feedback from staff and patrons to fine-tune AI tools.

Example: Update search algorithms based on user input regarding irrelevant search results.

3. Conduct Regular Training

Provide ongoing staff training to ensure they are equipped to manage and utilize expanded AI functionalities.

4. Collaborate with Vendors and Experts

Work with technology providers to implement updates and incorporate cutting-edge features.

Example: Partner with a vendor to add advanced natural language processing (NLP) capabilities to an AI-powered catalog.

5. Monitor Technological Trends

Stay informed about emerging AI technologies to incorporate innovative solutions into library operations.

Example: Explore AI-driven immersive technologies like augmented reality (AR) for enhanced user engagement.

4. Overcoming Challenges in Scaling and Improvement

Resource Constraints

Challenge: Limited budgets or staff expertise can hinder scaling efforts.

Solution: Use phased implementation and prioritize high-impact, cost-effective solutions.

Resistance to Change

Challenge: Staff or patrons may resist expanded AI applications.

Solution: Communicate benefits, provide training, and address concerns transparently.

Data Privacy Concerns

Challenge: Increased AI applications may raise user privacy issues.

Solution: Strengthen data protection policies and ensure compliance with regulations.

Technical Complexity

Challenge: Expanding AI systems can introduce integration challenges.

Solution: Use scalable, modular systems that integrate seamlessly with existing infrastructure.

5. Measuring Success in Scaling and Continuous Improvement

Adoption Rates:

Track usage of newly scaled AI tools.

Performance Metrics:

Measure efficiency improvements, such as reduced response times or increased resource utilization.

User Satisfaction:

Monitor feedback to assess the impact of new features and refinements.

Operational Efficiency:

Evaluate time and cost savings achieved through expanded AI functionalities.

6. Case Study: Scaling Up AI-Powered Accessibility Tools

A university library initially implemented text-to-speech tools for digital collections. Based on positive feedback, the library scaled the tools to include physical materials using scanning and OCR (optical character recognition) technologies. Continuous feedback revealed a need for language translation features, which were subsequently added. Over two years, the adoption rate for accessibility tools increased by 50%, and user satisfaction scores rose significantly.

7. Benefits of Scaling Up and Continuous Improvement

Broader Impact:

Extends the benefits of AI across more services and user groups.

Increased Efficiency:

Optimized workflows and automated processes reduce manual effort.

Enhanced User Engagement:

Improved tools and expanded functionalities keep users actively engaged.

Future-Readiness:

Positions the library as a forward-thinking institution prepared to adopt emerging technologies.

In conclusion, scaling up and continuous improvement are essential for maximizing the impact of AI-powered solutions in libraries. By expanding the scope of AI applications and refining their functionality based on data and feedback, libraries can achieve sustained innovation, efficiency, and user satisfaction.

Part IV: Case Studies and Best Practices
Chapter 14: Success Stories from Early Adopters

Interviews with Library Leaders

Interviews with library leaders who have successfully implemented AI technologies provide valuable insights into the transformative potential of AI in libraries. These firsthand accounts highlight the strategies, challenges, and outcomes of AI adoption, offering practical lessons and inspiration for other libraries. By examining these success stories, libraries can better understand the real-world applications of AI, the benefits it delivers, and the best practices for achieving success.

1. Importance of Leader Insights

Real-World Applications:

Demonstrates how AI can address specific challenges and improve library operations.

Proven Strategies:

Offers actionable advice on planning, implementation, and scaling.

Challenges and Solutions:

Provides an honest look at obstacles faced during implementation and how they were overcome.

Inspiration for Innovation:

Motivates other libraries to embrace AI by showcasing tangible benefits and successful outcomes.

2. Common Themes from Interviews with Library Leaders

Identifying the Need for AI

Leaders often emphasize starting with a clear understanding of the library's challenges and user needs.

Example:

A university librarian cited a growing demand for personalized research support as the catalyst for implementing an AI-powered recommendation system.

Strategic Planning

Successful projects began with thorough planning and stakeholder engagement.

Insights:

o   "We involved our staff from day one, ensuring their input shaped the selection of AI tools."

o   "A detailed cost-benefit analysis helped secure funding from our administration."

3. Overcoming Resistance

Many leaders highlighted the importance of addressing staff and patron concerns about AI.

Quote:

"Transparency was key. We held open forums to explain how AI would augment, not replace, human roles in the library."

4. Implementation Challenges

Leaders often faced technical and logistical challenges, such as system integration or data inconsistencies.

Solutions:

o "Partnering with a reliable vendor was critical for navigating technical hurdles."

o "We standardized metadata before deploying the AI-powered cataloging tool, ensuring compatibility with our existing system."

5. Success Metrics

Measuring the impact of AI tools was a common priority.

Example Metrics:

o Increase in user engagement with digital resources.

o Reduction in staff workload for repetitive tasks.

o Positive feedback from patrons about new services.

Success Stories from AI Implementation

Case Study 1: Public Library Implements AI Chatbot

Leader Insight:

"Our chatbot handled over 80% of routine inquiries within the first six months, freeing up staff for more complex tasks."

Challenges: Initial skepticism from staff.

Solution: Comprehensive training and live demonstrations during rollout.

Case Study 2: University Library Enhances Search and Discovery

Leader Insight:

"The AI-powered search engine improved resource discovery by analyzing user queries in natural language, making our catalog more intuitive."

Results:

A 40% increase in resource usage and a significant reduction in user complaints about search difficulty.

Case Study 3: Regional Consortium Adopts Predictive Analytics

Leader Insight:

"By pooling data from member libraries, we used AI to predict resource demand, optimizing acquisitions and reducing redundancy."

Outcome:

Saved $100,000 in collective purchasing costs across the consortium in the first year.

Best Practices Highlighted by Library Leaders

Engage Stakeholders Early:

Include staff and patrons in the decision-making process to foster buy-in and support.

Start Small and Scale:

Pilot AI solutions in specific areas before expanding across services.

Prioritize Training:

Equip staff with the skills to manage and use AI tools effectively.

Monitor and Iterate:

Regularly evaluate performance and refine tools based on feedback.

Build Partnerships:

Collaborate with technology vendors and other libraries to share knowledge and resources.

Impact of Leader Insights on AI Adoption

Encourages Innovation:

Hearing success stories inspires other libraries to explore AI possibilities.

Minimizes Risks:

Learning from challenges faced by early adopters helps other libraries avoid common pitfalls.

Enhances Strategic Planning:

Practical advice informs effective goal-setting, budgeting, and implementation strategies.

Strengthens Advocacy:

Real-world examples support funding proposals and stakeholder engagement efforts.

Conclusion

Interviews with library leaders who have implemented AI provide a wealth of knowledge and inspiration for libraries embarking on similar journeys. Their insights underscore the importance of clear planning, stakeholder engagement, and continuous refinement in achieving AI-powered success.

Key Lessons Learned

The experiences of early adopters of AI in libraries provide crucial insights into the successes and challenges of integrating AI-powered tools and services. By examining these key lessons, libraries can better prepare for their own AI journeys, avoiding common pitfalls and leveraging proven strategies to achieve their goals. These lessons highlight the importance of clear planning, stakeholder collaboration, and a commitment to continuous improvement.

1. Lessons in Planning and Preparation

Align AI Initiatives with Strategic Goals

Early adopters emphasize the importance of ensuring that AI projects align with the library's mission and priorities.

Lesson: Clearly define how AI will enhance user experience, streamline operations, or improve access to resources.

Example: A public library successfully implemented a chatbot by aligning it with the goal of improving patron support and reducing staff workload.

2. Conduct Thorough Needs Assessments

Comprehensive needs assessments help identify the most impactful use cases for AI.

Lesson: Understand user needs, operational inefficiencies, and resource constraints before selecting AI tools.

Example: A university library chose to prioritize AI-driven search enhancements after identifying user frustration with complex catalog systems.

2. Lessons in Implementation

Start Small and Scale Gradually

Pilot projects allow for controlled testing and iterative improvements.

Lesson: Begin with a targeted implementation in one area, gather feedback, and expand based on results.

Example: A consortium of libraries piloted predictive analytics for resource management with a single member library before scaling to the entire group.

Engage Stakeholders Early

Including staff, patrons, and leadership in the planning and implementation phases fosters support and reduces resistance.

Lesson: Create opportunities for stakeholder input to build trust and collaboration.

Example: A library involved staff in selecting an AI cataloging tool, addressing concerns about automation replacing human expertise.

Address Data and Integration Challenges

Integration with existing systems and data quality are common hurdles.

Lesson: Invest in data cleanup and ensure compatibility between AI tools and legacy systems.

Example: A public library standardized its metadata before deploying an AI-driven classification tool, ensuring accurate and consistent results.

3. Lessons in User Experience

Focus on Accessibility and Inclusivity

AI solutions should cater to diverse user needs, including those with disabilities or language barriers.

Lesson: Prioritize accessibility features and test tools with diverse user groups.

Example: A library integrated text-to-speech and translation capabilities into its AI-powered catalog to better serve multilingual and visually impaired patrons.

Provide Comprehensive Training and Support

Both staff and patrons need guidance to use AI tools effectively.

Lesson: Offer training sessions, tutorials, and ongoing support to ensure successful adoption.

Example: A library provided hands-on workshops for staff and video tutorials for patrons to introduce its AI chatbot.

4. Lessons in Evaluation and Iteration

Measure Impact with Clear Metrics

Defining and tracking performance metrics ensures that AI projects deliver value.

Lesson: Establish KPIs and regularly review them to assess success and guide refinements.

Example: A library used metrics like chatbot response times and user satisfaction scores to measure the success of its pilot program.

Act on Feedback

Continuous improvement is driven by user and staff input.

Lesson: Create feedback loops to identify pain points and opportunities for enhancement.

Example: After gathering feedback, a library refined its AI-powered recommendation engine to provide more relevant suggestions.

Maintain and Update Systems

AI tools require regular updates and maintenance to remain effective.

Lesson: Allocate resources for ongoing monitoring, retraining models, and addressing emerging challenges.

Example: A university library partnered with its AI vendor to roll out periodic updates for its predictive analytics platform.

5. Lessons in Overcoming Challenges

Address Resistance to Change

Resistance from staff or patrons can slow adoption.

Lesson: Use transparent communication to highlight the benefits of AI and address concerns about job displacement or usability.

Example: A library hosted open forums to explain how AI tools would enhance, not replace, staff roles.

Prioritize Privacy and Security

Data privacy and security are critical in AI implementations.

Lesson: Build trust by adhering to data protection regulations and being transparent about data usage.

Example: A library implemented strict data encryption protocols and communicated them clearly to users.

6. Best Practices from Early Adopters

Create a Roadmap:

Develop a detailed implementation plan with timelines, milestones, and responsibilities.

Leverage Partnerships:

Collaborate with vendors, other libraries, and industry experts for guidance and support.

Celebrate Early Wins:

Highlight successes during pilot projects to build momentum and secure stakeholder buy-in.

Stay User-Centric:

Keep user needs at the center of AI initiatives, ensuring tools are intuitive and accessible.

7. Impact of Key Lessons

By learning from the experiences of early adopters, libraries can:

- Reduce risks and improve efficiency during implementation.

- Achieve higher adoption rates among staff and patrons.

- Deliver impactful services that align with their mission and user needs.

- Build a culture of innovation and adaptability.

Conclusion

The lessons learned from early adopters of AI in libraries provide invaluable guidance for institutions planning their own AI initiatives. From strategic planning to continuous improvement, these insights highlight the importance of collaboration, user focus, and adaptability.

Operational and Service-Level Impacts

Early adopters of AI technologies in libraries have demonstrated how these innovations can significantly enhance both operational efficiency and service quality. By automating repetitive tasks, optimizing resource management, and personalizing user interactions, AI-powered solutions enable libraries to meet evolving demands while maintaining a high standard of service. These success stories highlight the transformative potential of AI in streamlining operations, enriching user experiences, and achieving strategic objectives.

1. Operational Impacts of AI in Libraries

Enhanced Efficiency

Automation of Routine Tasks:

AI-powered tools reduce manual workloads, freeing staff to focus on strategic initiatives.

Example: A university library implemented an AI-driven classification system, reducing cataloging time by 40% and eliminating errors associated with manual data entry.

Streamlined Inventory Management:

Predictive analytics optimize resource allocation and reduce shortages.

Example: A public library used AI to track borrowing trends, enabling just-in-time acquisitions and saving $20,000 annually in procurement costs.

2. Cost Savings

AI reduces labor-intensive processes, leading to significant cost savings over time.

Example: An academic library implemented an AI chatbot, cutting the need for additional staff during peak inquiry periods and saving $50,000 annually in staffing costs.

3. Data-Driven Decision-Making

AI tools analyze large datasets to provide actionable insights for library management.

Example: A regional library consortium used AI-driven analytics to assess underutilized resources, redistributing them to higher-demand branches and increasing circulation rates by 25%.

4. Improved Resource Utilization

AI enhances space and resource management by predicting demand patterns.

Example: A library used occupancy sensors powered by AI to identify low-traffic study areas, enabling better space utilization and scheduling adjustments.

Service-Level Impacts of AI in Libraries

Improved User Experience

Personalized Recommendations:

AI recommendation systems enhance resource discovery by suggesting materials tailored to user preferences.

Example: A digital library deployed an AI-powered recommendation engine, leading to a 30% increase in user engagement with eBooks.

Faster Service Delivery:

Chatbots and virtual assistants provide instant responses to routine inquiries.

Example: A public library's AI chatbot handled 85% of user questions within 15 seconds, reducing wait times and increasing patron satisfaction.

Enhanced Accessibility

Inclusive Tools:

AI-powered accessibility features, such as text-to-speech and language translation, expand library services to underserved communities.

Example: A community library introduced text-to-speech tools for visually impaired users, resulting in a 40% increase in digital resource usage among this group.

Multilingual Support:

AI tools enable libraries to serve diverse populations by providing language translation for materials and inquiries.

Example: An urban library implemented AI translation tools, improving service delivery for non-English-speaking patrons by 50%.

Continuous Availability

AI-powered systems, such as chatbots, offer 24/7 support, ensuring round-the-clock access to library services.

Example: A college library's chatbot provided after-hours assistance, resolving 70% of queries outside of normal operating hours.

Enhanced Engagement with Patrons

AI facilitates interactive and engaging user experiences.

Example: A library used AI-powered gamification in its digital catalog, encouraging users to explore new genres and increasing catalog interactions by 25%.

Long-Term Impacts of AI on Library Operations and Services

Scalability

Libraries can expand their services without proportional increases in staff or resources.

Example: An AI-powered automated lending system allowed a suburban library to handle a 20% increase in circulation without hiring additional staff.

Adaptability to Future Needs

AI enables libraries to remain responsive to emerging trends and patron expectations.

Example: Library integrated AI-driven data analytics to identify new programming opportunities, such as STEM-focused workshops, based on patron interests.

Enhanced Competitiveness

AI positions libraries as innovative institutions, attracting more patrons and funding opportunities.

Example: A public library's use of AI for digital preservation earned recognition from local government, leading to increased funding for further technological upgrades.

Challenges and Solutions Highlighted by Early Adopters

Integration with Legacy Systems

Challenge: Compatibility issues between AI tools and existing infrastructure.

Solution: Use middleware solutions and phased implementation approaches to ensure smooth integration.

Staff Training Needs

Challenge: Ensuring staff can effectively use and manage AI tools.

Solution: Provide ongoing training programs and vendor support to build staff expertise.

Data Privacy Concerns

Challenge: Protecting user data while leveraging AI analytics.

Solution: Implement robust encryption protocols and adhere to privacy regulations.

5. Success Stories Highlighting Operational and Service-Level Impacts

Case Study 1: Public Library Enhances Patron Support

Implementation: An AI chatbot was deployed to answer FAQs and assist with catalog searches.

Impact:

o 85% of queries resolved without staff intervention.

o Patron satisfaction scores increased by 20%.

Case Study 2: University Library Optimizes Resource Discovery

Implementation: AI-driven semantic search was integrated into the library's catalog.

Impact:

o Search success rates improved by 35%.

o User feedback indicated a significant reduction in frustration with finding resources.

Conclusion

The operational and service-level impacts demonstrated by early adopters of AI in libraries highlight the transformative potential of these technologies. From streamlining workflows to delivering personalized, accessible, and responsive services, AI empowers libraries to meet the needs of modern users while optimizing resource utilization.

Chapter 15: Ethical and Privacy Considerations

<u>AI Ethics in Public Institutions</u>

As public institutions, libraries have a profound responsibility to uphold ethical standards when implementing AI technologies. The use of AI in libraries intersects with key ethical considerations such as data privacy, inclusivity, transparency, and accountability. Addressing these considerations is critical to maintaining public trust, ensuring equitable access, and fostering a safe and welcoming environment for all patrons. Early adopters of AI in libraries provide valuable insights into the challenges and best practices for navigating these ethical dimensions.

1. The Role of Ethics in AI-Powered Libraries

Preserving Trust

Libraries are trusted institutions, and ethical missteps with AI could undermine public confidence.

Key Point: Transparent communication about how AI works and its implications builds trust.

Protecting Privacy

Libraries often handle sensitive patron data, such as borrowing history and personal information.

Key Point: Strong privacy safeguards and adherence to data protection regulations are essential.

Ensuring Fairness and Inclusivity

AI systems can inadvertently reflect or amplify biases present in their training data.

Key Point: Libraries must actively mitigate biases to provide equitable access and services.

Aligning with Public Values

As publicly funded institutions, libraries have an obligation to align AI usage with the values of transparency, accountability, and community benefit.

2. Ethical Challenges in Implementing AI in Public Libraries

Data Privacy and Consent

Challenge: Ensuring that user data is collected, stored, and used responsibly.

Example: Concerns about patron data being shared with third-party vendors for AI training purposes.

Solution:

o   Implement opt-in consent mechanisms for data collection.

o   Use anonymized or aggregated data to train AI systems.

Algorithmic Bias

Challenge: AI systems may produce biased recommendations or outputs based on skewed training data.

Example: An AI-powered recommendation system prioritizes popular genres over underrepresented ones, reducing access to diverse materials.

Solution:

o   Regularly audit algorithms for bias.

o   Incorporate diverse datasets and perspectives into training data.

3. Lack of Transparency

Challenge: Patrons and staff may not understand how AI tools make decisions.

Example: A chatbot provides inconsistent responses, leaving users confused about its logic.

Solution:

o   Use explainable AI models.

o   Offer clear documentation about how AI tools function and their limitations.

4. Digital Divide

Challenge: AI tools may inadvertently exclude users with limited digital literacy or access to technology.

Example: Patrons without smartphones cannot use a mobile-based AI service.

Solution:

o   Provide alternative access methods, such as physical kiosks or staff-assisted options.

o   Offer training sessions to enhance digital literacy among patrons.

Best Practices for Ethical AI Implementation in Public Libraries

Establish Clear Policies

Develop comprehensive AI ethics policies that address privacy, transparency, bias mitigation, and accountability.

Example: A library's AI policy explicitly states that patron data will not be shared with third parties without consent.

Engage Stakeholders

Involve patrons, staff, and community members in discussions about AI tools and their ethical implications.

Example: A library hosts public forums to gather feedback on planned AI implementations.

Regular Audits and Oversight

Conduct routine evaluations of AI systems to identify and rectify ethical concerns.

Example: Periodic audits reveal and address biases in an AI-powered recommendation system.

4. Foster Transparency and Education

Provide accessible information about how AI tools work and their potential impacts.

Example: Publish a guide explaining the library's chatbot technology, including how it handles user data.

Collaborate with Ethical AI Experts

Partner with experts in AI ethics to design and evaluate systems.

Example: A library works with a university AI ethics team to assess the fairness of its predictive analytics tools.

4. Case Studies: Ethical AI Implementation in Libraries

Case Study 1: Public Library Protects Patron Privacy

Challenge: Concerns over data collection by an AI-powered catalog search engine.

Action: The library implemented data anonymization protocols and provided an opt-out option for patrons.

Result: Increased patron trust and adoption of the search tool.

Case Study 2: University Library Mitigates Algorithmic Bias

Challenge: An AI recommendation system favored STEM resources over humanities content.

Action: The library diversified its training dataset and introduced manual curation for underrepresented fields.

Result: Balanced recommendations and higher user satisfaction.

Case Study 3: Community Library Addresses Digital Divide

Challenge: Older patrons struggled to use an AI chatbot.

Action: The library provided training sessions and introduced voice-activated options for chatbot interactions.

Result: Expanded accessibility and a 20% increase in chatbot usage among senior patrons.

5. Long-Term Benefits of Ethical AI Implementation

Sustained Trust:

Ethical practices reinforce the library's role as a trusted community institution.

Enhanced Inclusivity:

Equitable access ensures all patrons benefit from AI technologies.

Future-Readiness:

Transparent and responsible AI practices prepare libraries for evolving ethical and regulatory landscapes.

Community Empowerment:

Ethical AI fosters a sense of agency among patrons, ensuring they feel valued and respected.

Conclusion

AI ethics in public institutions like libraries are not just a responsibility but an opportunity to demonstrate leadership in using technology for social good. By addressing challenges such as data privacy, bias, and inclusivity, libraries can set a benchmark for ethical AI use in public services.

Protecting Patron Data

Protecting patron data is one of the most critical ethical considerations in implementing AI-powered technologies in libraries. As trusted institutions, libraries handle sensitive information about their patrons, including borrowing histories, personal preferences, and sometimes even demographic or financial details. Safeguarding this data ensures compliance with privacy regulations, maintains public trust, and fosters an ethical foundation for AI-driven innovation.

1. Importance of Data Privacy in Libraries

Trust and Reputation

Libraries are seen as safe havens for knowledge and information. Any breach of data privacy can significantly damage this trust.

Key Point: Demonstrating a commitment to privacy protection strengthens the library's reputation and patron loyalty.

Compliance with Legal Standards

Adherence to regulations such as GDPR (General Data Protection Regulation) and CCPA (California Consumer Privacy Act) is mandatory.

Key Point: Failure to comply with these laws can result in legal penalties and loss of funding.

Ethical Responsibility

Libraries have an ethical duty to protect users, particularly vulnerable populations, from potential misuse of their data.

2. Common Risks to Patron Data

Data Breaches

Unauthorized access to sensitive data due to insufficient security measures.

Example: Hackers accessing borrowing histories or personal details stored in AI systems.

Inappropriate Data Sharing

Sharing data with third-party vendors without explicit patron consent.

Example: An AI vendor using patron data for training algorithms without proper anonymization.

Insufficient Anonymization

Poorly anonymized data can still be traced back to individual patrons.

Example: Recommendations based on a user's borrowing history inadvertently revealing private interests.

Lack of Transparency

Patrons not understanding how their data is collected, used, or stored.

Example: An AI chatbot failing to disclose that it logs user interactions for analytics.

3. Best Practices for Protecting Patron Data

Data Minimization

Collect only the data necessary for the intended AI functionality.

Example: An AI recommendation system requiring only borrowing histories, not demographic data, to personalize suggestions.

Anonymization and Encryption

Ensure all stored data is anonymized to remove personally identifiable information (PII).

Example: Use hashing techniques to anonymize user IDs.

Encrypt data during storage and transmission to prevent unauthorized access.

Transparent Data Policies

Publish clear, accessible policies outlining how patron data is collected, used, and shared.

Example: A library's chatbot explicitly informs users that their interactions are logged for service improvement, but personal details remain confidential.

4. Consent-Based Data Collection

Seek explicit opt-in consent from patrons before collecting or using their data.

Example: Providing an option for users to decline participation in data-driven personalization services.

5. Vendor Oversight

- Collaborate only with vendors who adhere to strict data privacy standards.

- Include data protection clauses in contracts with AI providers.

Example: Requiring vendors to delete patron data after completing AI model training.

6. Regular Privacy Audits

Conduct audits to ensure compliance with privacy policies and regulations.

Example: Periodic reviews of data logs to verify adherence to anonymization practices.

Success Stories of Patron Data Protection

Case Study 1: Public Library Implements Robust Encryption

Challenge: Protecting sensitive borrowing data from potential breaches.

Solution: Implemented end-to-end encryption for all patron records.

Outcome: No reported breaches since implementation, increasing user confidence in digital services.

Case Study 2: University Library Enforces Vendor Compliance

Challenge: Ensuring third-party vendors respect data privacy.

Solution: Required vendors to comply with GDPR and conduct regular data deletion audits.

Outcome: Strengthened partnerships and improved patron trust in AI-powered tools.

Case Study 3: Community Library Adopts Transparent Policies

Challenge: Addressing patron concerns about data usage by an AI chatbot.

Solution: Published an FAQ detailing data collection practices and gave patrons the ability to opt out.

Outcome: Increased chatbot adoption rates and positive feedback about transparency.

Benefits of Robust Data Protection Practices

1. **Strengthened Trust**:

o   Reassures patrons that their data is safe, fostering loyalty and engagement.

2. **Regulatory Compliance**:

o   Protects libraries from legal risks and potential fines.

3. **Ethical Leadership**:

o   Positions the library as a role model for responsible data use in public institutions.

4. **Enhanced Service Adoption**:

o   Transparent data practices encourage more patrons to utilize AI-powered tools.

Conclusion

Protecting patron data is not just a legal requirement but an ethical imperative for AI-powered libraries. By implementing best practices such as data minimization, encryption, and transparent policies, libraries can safeguard user information while leveraging AI to enhance services. Success stories from early adopters highlight the effectiveness of these strategies, offering a roadmap for libraries to navigate the complex intersection of innovation and privacy.

Designing AI Systems

Transparency and accountability are essential principles for ethical AI implementation in libraries. As trusted public institutions, libraries must ensure that their AI systems operate in a clear, explainable, and responsible manner. This approach fosters trust, mitigates concerns about data misuse, and ensures that AI tools align with the values of fairness, inclusivity, and user empowerment. Designing AI systems with these principles in mind not only enhances their effectiveness but also reinforces the library's reputation as a community-centric institution.

1. Importance of Transparency and Accountability

Builds Trust

Transparency in how AI systems operate and use data reassures patrons that their interests are prioritized.

Ensures Ethical Compliance

Accountability mechanisms ensure adherence to ethical guidelines and legal standards.

Promotes Inclusivity

Transparent AI designs allow libraries to identify and address biases, ensuring equitable services.

Facilitates User Understanding and Empowerment

Clear explanations of AI processes enable patrons to make informed decisions about their interactions with library systems.

2. Key Principles for Transparent and Accountable AI Systems

Explainability

Ensure that the logic and processes behind AI decisions are understandable to users and staff.

Example: A recommendation system provides users with reasons for suggested resources, such as "Recommended based on your recent borrowing history."

Open Communication

Clearly communicate AI system capabilities, limitations, and how data is utilized.

Example: A chatbot includes a disclaimer that states, "This system logs interactions to improve service but does not store personal details."

3. Bias Mitigation

Design AI systems to minimize biases in algorithms and outputs.

Example: Regularly audit training data to ensure diversity in content and prevent algorithmic favoritism.

4. User Control

Provide users with options to opt out of AI-driven features or customize their interactions.

Example: Allow patrons to disable personalized recommendations in catalog searches.

5. Accountability Mechanisms

Establish clear processes for addressing errors, biases, or misuse of AI systems.

Example: Implement a reporting system for users to flag inaccurate or inappropriate AI-generated responses.

Steps to Design Transparent and Accountable AI Systems

Conduct a Needs Assessment

Identify the specific user and operational needs that the AI system will address.

Example: Assess whether patrons require more personalized resource recommendations or faster response times for inquiries.

Involve Stakeholders Early

Collaborate with staff, patrons, and technology experts to incorporate diverse perspectives into AI system design.

Select Ethical Vendors

Partner with vendors who prioritize ethical AI development, transparency, and accountability.

Example: Choose vendors that provide clear documentation of their algorithms and data handling practices.

Implement Explainable AI (XAI)

Use AI models that can explain their decisions and outputs in simple, user-friendly terms.

Develop Comprehensive Documentation

Create detailed guides for staff and patrons that outline how the AI system functions, its benefits, and its limitations.

Monitor and Audit Regularly

Continuously evaluate AI system performance to ensure transparency and accountability standards are upheld.

Case Studies: Transparent and Accountable AI in Libraries

Case Study 1: Public Library's Transparent Chatbot

Challenge: Patrons expressed concerns about data privacy when interacting with a chatbot.

Solution: The library implemented a chatbot with real-time notifications explaining data usage and gave users the option to opt out of data logging.

Outcome: Increased patron trust and a 30% rise in chatbot interactions.

Case Study 2: Academic Library's Bias-Free Recommendation System

Challenge: Initial testing revealed that the AI recommendation system disproportionately favored resources from STEM fields.

Solution: The library diversified the training dataset and introduced a feature allowing users to customize recommendation categories.

Outcome: Balanced recommendations and improved user satisfaction.

Case Study 3: Regional Consortium's Accountability Framework

Challenge: Member libraries raised concerns about the lack of accountability in predictive analytics used for resource allocation.

Solution: The consortium created a centralized committee to oversee AI system audits and address flagged issues.

Outcome: Improved transparency and equitable resource distribution across member libraries.

Benefits of Transparent and Accountable AI Systems

Enhanced User Trust:

Patrons feel confident using AI tools when they understand how they work.

Improved System Reliability:

Regular audits and clear processes for error correction ensure AI systems remain accurate and unbiased.

Greater Adoption Rates:

Transparent practices encourage wider use of AI tools among patrons and staff.

Alignment with Ethical Standards:

Accountability measures reinforce the library's commitment to ethical service delivery.

Challenges and Solutions in Implementing Transparency and Accountability

Challenge: Complexity of AI Systems

Solution: Use simpler, explainable algorithms and provide user-friendly documentation.

Challenge: Resistance to Change

Solution: Educate staff and patrons about the benefits of transparent and accountable AI practices.

Challenge: Resource Limitations

Solution: Partner with ethical AI vendors and seek grant funding for system audits and improvements.

Conclusion

Designing AI systems for transparency and accountability is essential for libraries to maintain their role as ethical and trusted public institutions. By prioritizing explainability, open communication, and robust accountability mechanisms, libraries can ensure that their AI-powered tools serve patrons equitably and responsibly. The experiences of early adopters demonstrate that transparent and accountable AI systems enhance user trust, improve system performance, and align with the core mission of libraries to provide inclusive and reliable access to information.

Chapter 16: Future Directions for AI in Libraries

Emerging Technologies

Emerging technologies such as augmented reality (AR), virtual reality (VR), robotics, and advanced natural language processing (NLP) are shaping the future of libraries by redefining how information is accessed, delivered, and experienced. These innovations expand the scope of AI applications in libraries, enabling immersive learning, interactive services, and more intuitive interactions. By integrating these technologies, libraries can transform their spaces into dynamic hubs of knowledge, creativity, and engagement.

1. Augmented Reality (AR) and Virtual Reality (VR)

Enhancing User Experience

AR and VR provide immersive and interactive ways for patrons to engage with library resources.

Applications:

o **Virtual Tours**: Patrons can explore library collections, archives, or exhibits through VR experiences.

o **AR-Enhanced Catalogs**: Patrons use AR-enabled devices to visualize book locations or access additional content in real time.

Example:

A university library implemented VR to allow students to explore ancient historical sites as part of their research projects.

Supporting Learning and Research

AR/VR technologies create experiential learning opportunities.

Applications:

o VR simulations for medical or engineering students.

o   AR tools for language learning, where virtual objects interact with spoken or written language.

Example:

A public library introduced VR-based STEM programs for children, significantly boosting attendance in educational workshops.

Challenges and Solutions

Challenges:

o   High costs of equipment and development.

o   Accessibility for patrons with limited technical skills.

Solutions:

o   Partner with educational institutions or technology companies to offset costs.

o   Provide staff training and user-friendly tutorials for patrons.

2. Robotics in Libraries

Automating Routine Tasks

Robotics can streamline operations such as shelving, inventory management, and material delivery.

Applications:

o   Automated guided vehicles (AGVs) for book transportation.

o   Robotic systems for efficient inventory checks.

Example:

A large city library deployed a robotic shelving system that reduced book retrieval times by 50%.

Enhancing Patron Interactions

Robots can serve as interactive assistants, providing information or guiding patrons.

Applications:

o   AI-driven robots answering FAQs or helping patrons navigate the library.

o   Interactive storytelling sessions for children led by humanoid robots.

Example:

A library in Japan introduced a humanoid robot to greet patrons and assist with locating books, increasing user satisfaction.

Challenges and Solutions

Challenges:

o   High initial investment and maintenance costs.

o   Limited capability to handle complex tasks.

Solutions:

o   Implement robotics in phases, starting with simpler tasks.

o   Collaborate with robotics researchers to develop customized solutions.

3. Advanced Natural Language Processing (NLP)

Enabling Intuitive Interactions

Advanced NLP enhances communication between patrons and AI systems.

Applications:

o Chatbots with conversational abilities that mimic human interactions.

o Voice-activated search tools for accessibility and convenience.

Example:

o A public library implemented an NLP-powered chatbot that understood regional dialects, improving service accessibility.

Improving Information Discovery

NLP tools enable semantic search, making information retrieval more accurate and user-friendly.

Applications:

o Context-aware search engines that understand user intent.

o Tools that summarize large documents or extract key insights.

Example:

o An academic library used NLP to create a tool that summarized research papers, saving time for students and researchers.

Challenges and Solutions

Challenges:

o Potential biases in NLP algorithms.

o Technical complexities in implementing advanced models.

Solutions:

o Regularly audit NLP models to detect and correct biases.

o Use pre-trained models and collaborate with NLP experts for smoother integration.

4. Integration of Emerging Technologies

Creating Immersive Learning Spaces

Combining AR/VR with robotics and NLP can turn libraries into futuristic learning hubs.

Example:

A library creates an AI-driven learning lab where patrons can use VR for immersive history lessons, robots for hands-on STEM activities, and NLP tools for real-time language translation.

Enhancing Accessibility

Emerging technologies can make library services more inclusive.

Example:

NLP-powered voice assistants combined with AR visual aids help visually impaired users navigate the library.

5. Case Studies: Libraries Embracing Emerging Technologies

Case Study 1: Virtual Reality in Academic Libraries

Implementation: A university library launched VR stations for experiential learning in fields like archaeology and engineering.

Outcome: Increased student engagement and innovative use of library spaces for research.

Case Study 2: Robotics in Public Libraries

Implementation: A public library used robots to guide patrons and automate inventory management.

Outcome: Reduced operational costs and improved service delivery efficiency.

Case Study 3: Advanced NLP for Enhanced Discovery

Implementation: A library integrated semantic search powered by NLP into its catalog system.

Outcome: A 40% increase in successful search queries and a significant reduction in user frustration.

6. Challenges and Opportunities

Challenges

- High implementation and maintenance costs.

- Ensuring inclusivity and accessibility.

- Addressing ethical concerns, such as data privacy.

Opportunities

- Increased engagement through immersive experiences.

- Enhanced operational efficiency and resource management.

- Expansion of services to diverse user groups.

Conclusion

Emerging technologies like AR/VR, robotics, and advanced NLP are reshaping the landscape of library services and operations. By integrating these innovations, libraries can create immersive, interactive, and inclusive environments that meet the needs of modern users. While challenges remain, the success stories of early adopters demonstrate the transformative potential of these technologies.

Anticipating Challenges and Opportunities

As libraries continue to adopt AI technologies, understanding and preparing for the associated challenges and opportunities is essential. While AI offers transformative potential to enhance library operations, user experience, and resource accessibility, it also introduces complexities such as ethical dilemmas, technical barriers, and resource constraints. Proactively addressing these challenges and leveraging emerging opportunities enables libraries to navigate the evolving technological landscape effectively and equitably.

1. Key Challenges in Implementing AI in Libraries

Ethical Concerns

- **Challenge**: Ensuring AI systems align with the library's ethical commitments, such as protecting user privacy and avoiding biases.

- **Example**: Algorithms trained on biased datasets may unintentionally exclude certain user groups.

- **Mitigation**: Regular audits, diverse training datasets, and robust ethical guidelines ensure AI systems uphold fairness and transparency.

2. Resource Constraints

- **Challenge**: High costs of implementing and maintaining AI technologies can strain budgets, especially for smaller libraries.

- **Example**: Limited funding restricts access to advanced AI tools or hardware.

- **Mitigation**: Libraries can explore grants, partnerships, and shared resources within consortia to reduce costs.

3. Integration Complexities

- **Challenge**: Seamlessly integrating AI tools with existing library management systems and workflows.

- **Example**: Difficulty in aligning an AI-powered recommendation engine with legacy catalog systems.

- **Mitigation**: Collaborate with vendors to ensure compatibility and invest in phased implementation approaches.

4. Skills Gap

- **Challenge**: Lack of staff expertise in AI technology may hinder effective adoption and usage.

- **Example**: Library staff may feel unprepared to manage or troubleshoot AI systems.

- **Mitigation**: Provide ongoing training, workshops, and vendor support to build staff confidence and expertise.

5. Public Perception and Resistance

- **Challenge**: Users and staff may resist AI adoption due to concerns about job displacement, data privacy, or trust in technology.

- **Example**: Patrons may be reluctant to use an AI chatbot, preferring human interaction.

- **Mitigation**: Transparent communication about AI's role, benefits, and safeguards can help address these concerns.

Opportunities for AI-Driven Transformation in Libraries

1. Enhancing User Experience

- AI-powered tools can personalize and streamline patron interactions.

- **Example**: Chatbots providing instant assistance or recommendation systems tailored to individual preferences increase user engagement and satisfaction.

2. Expanding Accessibility

- AI technologies can make library services more inclusive for diverse user groups.

- **Example**: Text-to-speech tools and language translation systems enhance access for visually impaired or non-native-speaking patrons.

3. Optimizing Operations

- AI can automate routine tasks, enabling staff to focus on strategic initiatives.

- **Example**: Automated inventory management and predictive analytics streamline resource allocation and reduce inefficiencies.

4. Innovating Learning Spaces

- AI technologies like augmented reality (AR), virtual reality (VR), and robotics create immersive and interactive learning opportunities.

- **Example**: A library introduces VR-based STEM education programs to engage young learners.

5. Leveraging Data for Insights

- AI analytics can provide actionable insights into user behavior, resource usage, and community needs.

- **Example**: Libraries use predictive models to forecast demand for specific resources, optimizing acquisitions and programming.

Strategies for Navigating Challenges and Opportunities

1. Proactive Planning

- Anticipate challenges by conducting thorough needs assessments and engaging stakeholders early.

- **Example**: A library forms a task force to evaluate potential ethical issues before implementing AI tools.

2. Collaboration and Partnerships

- Partner with technology providers, academic institutions, and other libraries to share expertise, resources, and costs.

- **Example**: Libraries within a regional consortium collaborate to develop and share an AI-powered cataloging system.

3. Phased Implementation

- Roll out AI initiatives incrementally, starting with pilot projects to address potential issues and gather feedback.

- **Example**: Deploy an AI chatbot in a single department before expanding it across the library.

4. Continuous Learning and Adaptation

- Stay updated on emerging AI technologies and trends to remain competitive and future-ready.

- **Example**: Attend conferences, participate in webinars, and engage with AI research to explore new opportunities.

5. Community-Centric Approach

- Ensure AI initiatives align with the community's values and needs.

- **Example**: Host public forums to gather input on AI services, ensuring they reflect local priorities and concerns.

4. Case Studies: Anticipating and Overcoming Challenges

Case Study 1: Addressing Ethical Concerns

- **Challenge**: A public library faced criticism for implementing a recommendation system that some users found biased.

- **Solution**: Conducted an independent audit of the algorithm, diversified training data, and introduced transparency reports.

- **Outcome**: Restored user trust and improved recommendation accuracy.

Case Study 2: Overcoming Resource Constraints

- **Challenge**: A small library struggled with limited funding for an AI chatbot.

- **Solution**: Partnered with a local university to develop and maintain the system.

- **Outcome**: Successfully launched the chatbot, increasing user engagement by 25%.

Case Study 3: Expanding Accessibility

- **Challenge**: A rural library sought to serve non-English-speaking patrons more effectively.

- **Solution**: Integrated AI translation tools into its catalog and website.

- **Outcome**: Improved resource access for a previously underserved demographic.

Long-Term Benefits of Proactive Strategies

1. **Sustained Relevance**:

Libraries remain vital in an increasingly digital world by embracing and adapting to AI technologies.

2. **Improved Services**:

Enhanced user experiences through personalized and accessible offerings.

3. **Operational Efficiency**:

Streamlined processes free up resources for innovation and community engagement.

4. **Increased Inclusivity**:

AI tools ensure equitable access to services for all patrons.

5. **Community Empowerment**:

Libraries serve as leaders in leveraging technology for public benefit.

Conclusion

Anticipating challenges and opportunities is crucial for libraries seeking to integrate AI technologies effectively. While ethical, technical, and financial obstacles may arise, proactive planning, collaboration, and a user-centric approach enable libraries to overcome these hurdles and harness AI's transformative potential. By addressing challenges and capitalizing on emerging opportunities, libraries can solidify their role as innovative, inclusive, and indispensable community institutions.

Building a Culture of Innovation

The integration of AI technologies in libraries not only transforms services and operations but also fosters a culture of innovation. By embracing forward-thinking strategies and encouraging creativity, libraries can position themselves as leaders in technological and educational advancement. Building a culture of innovation empowers staff, engages patrons, and ensures the library remains a vital, dynamic institution capable of adapting to the rapidly evolving digital landscape.

Importance of a Culture of Innovation in Libraries

1. Enhances Relevance

- Libraries must continually evolve to meet the changing needs of patrons in a technology-driven world.

- **Key Point**: An innovative culture enables libraries to remain relevant as centers of knowledge and community engagement.

2. Encourages Adaptability

- A culture of innovation ensures libraries can respond to emerging trends and challenges with agility.

- **Key Point**: Staff and leadership are more open to experimenting with and adopting new technologies.

3. Inspires Staff and Patron Engagement

- Innovation fosters excitement and collaboration among staff and patrons, creating a dynamic library environment.

- **Key Point**: Engaged staff are more likely to champion and sustain AI initiatives.

Strategies for Building a Culture of Innovation

1. Foster a Growth Mindset

- Encourage staff to view challenges as opportunities for learning and improvement.

- **Example**: Offer workshops on emerging AI trends and their potential applications in library operations.

2. Support Continuous Learning

- Provide access to training programs, conferences, and online resources to keep staff informed and skilled.

- **Example**: Partner with technology providers to deliver AI certification courses for library staff.

3. Promote Collaboration and Experimentation

- Create an environment where staff can collaborate and experiment with new ideas without fear of failure.

- **Example**: Establish innovation labs where staff can prototype AI-powered tools or services.

4. Recognize and Reward Innovation

- Acknowledge and reward staff contributions to innovative projects.

- **Example**: Host an annual "Innovation in Action" event to showcase successful AI initiatives.

5. Engage the Community

- Involve patrons in the innovation process to ensure new initiatives align with their needs and interests.

- **Example**: Conduct focus groups or hackathons to gather ideas for AI-powered services.

6. Embed Innovation in Organizational Values

- Include innovation as a core component of the library's mission and strategic goals.

- **Example**: Develop a five-year strategic plan that prioritizes technology-driven enhancements.

Examples of Libraries Cultivating Innovation

Case Study 1: Innovation Lab for Emerging Technologies

- **Implementation**: A university library created an innovation lab equipped with AI tools, VR headsets, and 3D printers.

- **Outcome**: Faculty and students collaborated to develop VR-based learning modules, enhancing educational experiences.

Case Study 2: Staff-Led AI Projects

- **Implementation**: A public library launched a staff innovation program, providing small grants for AI-related pilot projects.

- **Outcome**: Staff developed an AI chatbot for local history inquiries, which became a popular feature among patrons.

Case Study 3: Community Engagement Through Hackathons

- **Implementation**: A library hosted a hackathon inviting community members to design AI tools that enhance library services.

- **Outcome**: The event generated innovative ideas, including a mobile app for multilingual catalog searches.

Challenges in Building a Culture of Innovation

1. Resistance to Change

- **Challenge**: Staff and patrons may hesitate to adopt new technologies.

- **Solution**: Provide training and transparent communication about the benefits and impact of innovation.

2. Limited Resources

- **Challenge**: Financial and staffing constraints may limit the ability to experiment with new ideas.

- **Solution**: Partner with local businesses, universities, and technology providers to share costs and expertise.

3. Risk of Failure

- **Challenge**: Innovative projects may not always succeed.

- **Solution**: Foster a mindset that views failure as a learning opportunity and encourages iterative improvements.

Long-Term Benefits of a Culture of Innovation

1. Sustained Technological Advancement

Libraries that embrace innovation are better positioned to integrate emerging technologies like AI, AR/VR, and robotics.

2. Improved Patron Services

Innovative libraries offer cutting-edge, user-focused services that enhance patron satisfaction and engagement.

3. Empowered Staff

Staff in innovative environments are more motivated, skilled, and proactive in driving change.

4. Enhanced Community Impact

Libraries become leaders in local innovation ecosystems, contributing to educational and technological progress in their communities.

Conclusion

Building a culture of innovation is essential for libraries to thrive in the age of AI and beyond. By fostering creativity, encouraging collaboration, and embracing change, libraries can position themselves as leaders in technological and educational transformation. Success stories from early adopters illustrate the profound impact of such a culture, demonstrating how libraries can innovate not just in service delivery but also in their role as community anchors.

Summary of Key Takeaways

AI-Powered Libraries: A Practical Guide to Transforming Services and Operations provides a comprehensive framework for libraries to embrace the transformative potential of artificial intelligence. As libraries navigate the challenges and opportunities of the digital era, this guide underscores the importance of strategic planning, stakeholder engagement, ethical implementation, and continuous innovation. Below is a summary of the key takeaways that highlight how AI can revolutionize library services and operations.

1. The Evolving Role of Libraries in the AI Era

- Libraries are no longer just repositories of knowledge; they are dynamic hubs for learning, innovation, and community engagement.

- AI enables libraries to enhance accessibility, improve user experience, and optimize operational efficiency.

2. Foundations for AI Integration

- **Understanding AI**: Familiarity with AI concepts such as machine learning, natural language processing (NLP), and computer vision is essential.

- **Ethical Implications**: Addressing concerns such as data privacy, algorithmic bias, and transparency is critical to maintaining public trust.

- **Changing Library Services**: AI shifts traditional library operations, emphasizing digital resource management, personalization, and predictive analytics.

3. AI Tools and Technologies for Libraries

- **Conversational AI and Chatbots**: Enhancing patron support with 24/7 assistance and intuitive user interactions.

- **Intelligent Search and Discovery**: Revolutionizing resource discovery through semantic search and personalized recommendations.

- **Digital Preservation and Data Mining**: Utilizing AI to preserve archives and support data-driven research.

- **Accessibility Tools**: Expanding services for diverse user groups with speech-to-text, text-to-speech, and translation tools.

- **Operational Efficiency**: Streamlining workflows, improving resource management, and enhancing security through AI-driven solutions.

4. Step-by-Step Implementation Roadmap

- **Laying the Groundwork**: Conducting needs assessments, defining goals, and engaging stakeholders.

- **Planning and Budgeting**: Identifying AI tools, creating timelines, and conducting cost-benefit analyses.

- **Designing Pilot Projects**: Selecting focus areas, defining success metrics, and mitigating risks.

- **Implementation and Rollout**: Ensuring technical setup, staff training, and effective patron awareness strategies.

- **Evaluation and Iteration**: Measuring performance, gathering feedback, and scaling up with continuous improvement.

5. Case Studies and Best Practices

- Success stories from early adopters demonstrate the tangible benefits of AI in libraries, such as improved user engagement, operational savings, and innovative programming.

- Ethical and privacy considerations emphasize the importance of transparency, data protection, and accountability.

- Future directions for AI highlight emerging technologies like AR/VR, robotics, and advanced NLP, offering new ways to engage patrons and optimize services.

6. Future Directions and the Path Forward

- **Anticipating Challenges**: Addressing ethical, technical, and financial barriers with proactive strategies.

- **Building a Culture of Innovation**: Empowering staff and fostering creativity to drive sustained technological advancement.

- **Expanding Accessibility and Inclusivity**: Leveraging AI to ensure equitable access for all patrons, including underserved populations.

7. Key Benefits of AI in Libraries

- **Enhanced User Experience**: Personalized recommendations, faster assistance, and more intuitive search capabilities.

- **Operational Efficiency**: Automation of routine tasks and data-driven insights streamline workflows.

- **Inclusivity and Accessibility**: AI tools ensure services are accessible to diverse and marginalized communities.

- **Future-Readiness**: Libraries equipped with AI are better prepared to adapt to emerging technologies and changing user expectations.

Conclusion

AI offers libraries an unprecedented opportunity to transform their services, operations, and role within the community. While challenges such as resource constraints, ethical dilemmas, and technological complexities exist, the potential rewards - enhanced user experiences, operational efficiency, and greater accessibility - far outweigh the obstacles.

By adopting a strategic and proactive approach, libraries can lead the way in harnessing AI to meet the needs of the digital age.

Call to Action for Library Professionals

As the digital landscape continues to evolve, the integration of AI technologies in libraries is no longer a choice but a necessity. Library professionals stand at the forefront of this transformation, with a unique opportunity to shape the future of their institutions and the communities they serve. **AI-Powered Libraries: A Practical Guide to Transforming Services and Operations** emphasizes the critical role of library professionals in driving this change and calls on them to embrace innovation, lead with ethics, and collaborate for success.

1. Embrace the Potential of AI

Library professionals must recognize AI as a transformative tool to enhance services, optimize operations, and expand accessibility.

- **Key Action**: Explore AI applications that align with your library's mission, whether through personalized user services, automated cataloging, or predictive resource management.

- **Example**: Pilot an AI-powered chatbot to improve patron support and reduce staff workloads.

2. Lead with Vision and Ethics

The successful integration of AI requires strong leadership rooted in transparency, accountability, and ethical responsibility.

- **Key Action**: Develop and implement clear guidelines on data privacy, bias mitigation, and inclusive service delivery.

- **Example**: Create a data governance policy that ensures user data is protected and used responsibly.

3. Prioritize Collaboration and Learning

AI adoption is a collaborative effort that benefits from shared expertise and resources.

- **Key Action**: Partner with other libraries, educational institutions, and technology providers to share knowledge and reduce implementation costs.

- **Example**: Join regional consortia to develop shared AI-powered tools and resources.

4. Advocate for Innovation and Investment

Library professionals must champion the value of AI to stakeholders, securing the necessary funding and support for technological advancement.

- **Key Action**: Communicate the benefits of AI-powered services to funders, policymakers, and the community.

- **Example**: Present data-driven evidence of improved user satisfaction and operational efficiency from pilot AI projects.

5. Build a Culture of Experimentation

Innovation flourishes in environments where creativity and experimentation are encouraged.

- **Key Action**: Foster a growth mindset among staff by offering training, workshops, and opportunities to test new ideas.

- **Example**: Establish an innovation lab where staff and patrons can explore emerging technologies like VR, robotics, or NLP tools.

6. Address Challenges Proactively

Prepare for the challenges of AI integration, including ethical dilemmas, technical barriers, and public resistance.

- **Key Action**: Develop risk mitigation strategies and contingency plans for potential setbacks.

- **Example**: Conduct ethical audits of AI systems to identify and address biases or data privacy concerns.

7. Empower the Community

AI-powered libraries are not just about technology; they are about people. Ensure that AI tools serve as enablers of knowledge, inclusion, and empowerment.

- **Key Action**: Design AI-driven services that address the diverse needs of your community, including underserved populations.

- **Example**: Use AI translation tools to provide multilingual access to library resources.

8. Look to the Future

AI is a rapidly evolving field, and staying informed about emerging technologies is essential for sustained success.

- **Key Action**: Stay engaged with AI research, attend conferences, and network with innovators in the field.

- **Example**: Incorporate emerging technologies like AR/VR or predictive analytics into long-term strategic plans.

Call to Action

Library professionals are the architects of the future library experience. Embracing AI is not just about technology—it is about creating more inclusive, efficient, and innovative spaces where knowledge thrives.

- **Be Bold**: Take the first step toward AI adoption, whether through a pilot project or staff training program.

- **Be Ethical**: Lead with transparency and a commitment to serving all patrons equitably.

- **Be Collaborative**: Engage with partners, stakeholders, and the community to maximize the impact of AI initiatives.

- **Be Future-Focused**: Continuously learn, adapt, and innovate to keep libraries at the forefront of knowledge and technology.

By taking decisive action today, library professionals can ensure that their institutions remain vital, transformative, and indispensable in the digital age.

Appendices

Appendix A: AI Tools and Vendors Directory

Overview of Major Platforms and Software

Appendix A of **AI-Powered Libraries: A Practical Guide to Transforming Services and Operations** serves as a valuable resource for library professionals exploring the rapidly growing landscape of AI tools and vendors. This directory provides an overview of major platforms and software solutions tailored to the diverse needs of libraries, from resource management to user engagement and accessibility. Understanding the capabilities and specialties of these platforms enables libraries to make informed decisions, align technology choices with their goals, and implement solutions effectively.

AI Tools for Library Operations

1. Integrated Library Systems (ILS) with AI Features

- **Platforms**: Ex Libris Alma, Koha, and WorldShare Management Services (OCLC).

- **Capabilities**:

o Automated cataloging and metadata management.

o Predictive analytics for resource acquisition and collection management.

o AI-enhanced search functionalities.

- **Example**:

o Ex Libris Alma offers AI-powered analytics to optimize collection development and identify underutilized resources.

2. Workflow Automation

- **Platforms**: Springshare, LibAnswers, and LibChat.

- **Capabilities**:

o Automates repetitive tasks such as check-in/check-out and overdue notifications.

o Integrates chatbots for real-time user support.

- **Example**:

o Springshare's LibAnswers incorporates AI chatbots to handle FAQs, improving response times for patrons.

AI Tools for User Engagement and Support

1. Conversational AI and Chatbots

- **Platforms**: Dialogflow, IBM Watson Assistant, and Microsoft Bot Framework.

- **Capabilities**:

o Natural language understanding for intuitive patron interactions.

o Handles routine inquiries and redirects complex questions to staff.

- **Example**:

o IBM Watson Assistant is used by libraries to provide 24/7 support for catalog searches and service inquiries.

2. Personalized Recommendation Systems

- **Platforms**: OverDrive, Bibliotheca CloudLibrary, and EBSCOhost.

- **Capabilities**:

o AI-driven algorithms suggest books, articles, and other resources based on user preferences and behavior.

- **Example**:

o OverDrive leverages machine learning to recommend eBooks and audiobooks tailored to individual patron interests.

AI Tools for Resource Discovery

1. Semantic Search and Discovery Platforms

- **Platforms**: Primo (Ex Libris), VuFind, and BiblioCommons.
- **Capabilities**:

o Advanced search algorithms that understand user intent and context.

o Integrates keyword and natural language processing (NLP) for enhanced resource discovery.

- **Example**:

o VuFind uses semantic search to deliver more accurate and relevant search results in library catalogs.

2. Digital Archives and Preservation

- **Platforms**: Preservica, Archive-It, and Rosetta.
- **Capabilities**:

o AI-driven metadata extraction for efficient indexing and preservation.

o Automates long-term digital storage and access management.

- **Example**:

o Preservica's AI tools streamline the preservation of digital archives, ensuring accessibility over time.

AI Tools for Accessibility

1. Assistive Technologies

- **Platforms**: ReadSpeaker, JAWS, and NVDA.

- **Capabilities**:

o Text-to-speech, screen readers, and language translation to improve accessibility for visually impaired or multilingual users.

- **Example**:

o ReadSpeaker integrates with library catalogs to provide audio versions of text for patrons with visual impairments.

2. Speech and Language Processing Tools

- **Platforms**: Google Cloud Speech-to-Text, Amazon Polly, and Microsoft Azure Cognitive Services.

- **Capabilities**:

o Converts spoken language into text for transcription and analysis.

o Enhances multilingual support with real-time translation.

- **Example**:

o Google Cloud Speech-to-Text allows libraries to transcribe oral histories for inclusion in digital archives.

AI Tools for Advanced Analytics

1. Predictive Analytics Platforms

- **Platforms**: Tableau, Power BI, and QlikView.

- **Capabilities**:

o Data visualization and predictive modeling for resource management and programming.

- **Example**:

o Tableau provides visual analytics to forecast demand for specific collections and services.

2. User Behavior Analytics

- **Platforms**: Piwik PRO, Google Analytics 4, and Adobe Analytics.

- **Capabilities**:

o Tracks user interactions with digital platforms to identify trends and optimize services.

- **Example**:

o Piwik PRO is used to analyze digital catalog usage patterns, informing content acquisition decisions.

Choosing the Right AI Tool or Vendor

Key Considerations

- **Library Needs**: Identify specific challenges or goals that AI tools can address.

- **Scalability**: Ensure the tool can grow with the library's needs.

- **Vendor Reputation**: Work with vendors with a proven track record in library technology.

- **Integration**: Choose tools compatible with existing systems.

- **Cost and Support**: Evaluate pricing models and availability of vendor support.

Conclusion

The AI tools and platforms highlighted in Appendix A offer libraries a wide array of options to enhance their services and operations.

From automated cataloging and conversational AI to predictive analytics and accessibility tools, these technologies address diverse needs and enable libraries to thrive in a digital-first world. By carefully evaluating the capabilities and compatibility of these solutions, libraries can make strategic investments that align with their mission and drive innovation for years to come.

Comparison of Features and Costs

Appendix A of **AI-Powered Libraries: A Practical Guide to Transforming Services and Operations** provides a detailed comparison of features and costs associated with leading AI tools and platforms. Understanding these factors is crucial for library professionals seeking to maximize value while meeting operational and budgetary constraints. By analyzing the capabilities, pricing structures, and support services offered by various vendors, libraries can make informed decisions that align with their strategic goals.

Key Parameters for Comparison

1. Features

- **Scalability**: Tools that adapt to the library's growth or evolving needs.

- **Customization**: Ability to tailor the platform to specific library requirements.

- **Integration**: Compatibility with existing library management systems and workflows.

- **Advanced Capabilities**: AI-driven features such as natural language processing (NLP), predictive analytics, and automation.

2. Costs

- **Initial Setup Costs**: Licensing fees, hardware requirements, and implementation costs.

- **Subscription Models**: Annual or monthly pricing structures, often based on usage or user count.

- **Support and Maintenance**: Costs associated with updates, training, and technical support.

Comparative Overview of Major Platforms

1. Conversational AI and Chatbots

Platform	Key Features	Cost Structure	Examples of Use
Dialogflow	Multilingual NLP, custom intents, analytics tools.	Free tier; Paid plans starting at $0.002 per interaction.	FAQ bots, catalog search assistants.
IBM Watson Assistant	AI-driven dialogue, seamless integrations, voice support.	Custom pricing; typically starts at $140 per month.	24/7 patron support, multilingual bots.
Microsoft Bot Framework	Extensive API support, scalable cloud services.	Pay-as-you-go; variable based on usage.	Advanced virtual assistants for libraries.

2. AI-Powered Cataloging and Metadata Tools

Platform	Key Features	Cost Structure	Examples of Use
Ex Libris Alma	Automated metadata generation,	Subscription-based, starting at	Metadata creation,

Platform	Key Features	Cost Structure	Examples of Use
	analytics, resource sharing.	$15,000 annually for small libraries.	predictive analytics.
Koha	Open-source flexibility, community-driven enhancements.	Free (self-hosted); Hosting services start at $1,500 annually.	Open-source catalog management.
WorldShare (OCLC)	Shared cataloging, global data integration.	Custom pricing based on library size.	Collaborative resource management.

3. Resource Discovery Platforms

Platform	Key Features	Cost Structure	Examples of Use
Primo (Ex Libris)	Semantic search, customizable interfaces.	Custom pricing, typically starting at $20,000 annually.	Advanced search for academic libraries.
VuFind	Open-source, faceted searching, multilingual support.	Free; Hosting services available at variable costs.	Public library catalogs.
BiblioCommons	User-friendly design, community-	Subscription-based, pricing on request.	Public engagement platforms.

Platform	Key Features	Cost Structure	Examples of Use
	driven discovery.		

4. Accessibility Tools

Platform	Key Features	Cost Structure	Examples of Use
ReadSpeaker	Text-to-speech, multilingual support, browser integration.	Custom pricing based on scale and features.	Accessibility for digital catalogs.
JAWS	Screen reader with extensive keyboard navigation.	Licensing starts at $1,000 per user.	Accessibility for visually impaired patrons.
Amazon Polly	Real-time text-to-speech conversion.	Pay-as-you-go, starting at $4 per 1 million characters.	Audio versions of library resources.

5. Analytics Platforms

Platform	Key Features	Cost Structure	Examples of Use
Tableau	Interactive dashboards, predictive analytics.	Starting at $70 per user per month.	Usage trends, resource allocation.

Platform	Key Features	Cost Structure	Examples of Use
Power BI (Microsoft)	Seamless Microsoft integration, robust visualizations.	Free tier; Pro version at $10 per user per month.	Patron behavior analysis.
SAS Visual Analytics	Advanced AI models, machine learning integration.	Custom pricing based on usage and features.	Advanced data-driven decision-making.

Key Insights for Budgeting and Selection

1. Balancing Costs with Value

- Evaluate tools based on ROI, factoring in time saved, operational efficiency, and improved user satisfaction.

- **Example**: A chatbot with a moderate subscription cost may yield significant savings by reducing staff workloads.

2. Open-Source vs. Proprietary Solutions

- **Open-Source Advantage**: Flexibility and cost-effectiveness (e.g., Koha, VuFind).

- **Proprietary Tools**: Often offer more robust support and advanced features (e.g., Ex Libris Alma, Tableau).

3. Scalability and Long-Term Costs

- Choose platforms that can scale with the library's growth to avoid frequent transitions.

4. Benefits of Comparative Analysis

1. **Informed Decision-Making**:

o   Helps libraries identify platforms that align with their specific needs and budget.

2. **Optimized Investments**:

o   Ensures libraries achieve maximum value from AI tools while minimizing unnecessary expenditures.

3. **Enhanced Strategic Planning**:

o   Facilitates long-term planning by comparing features, costs, and scalability.

Conclusion

Appendix A's comparative analysis of AI tools and vendors equips libraries with the knowledge to make strategic investments in technology. By weighing features, costs, and use cases, library professionals can select platforms that deliver the greatest impact for their institutions. Whether optimizing workflows, enhancing user engagement, or expanding accessibility, these tools represent a pathway to innovation and efficiency.

Appendix B: Implementation Checklists

<u>Readiness Assessment Worksheet</u>

The **Readiness Assessment Worksheet** in Appendix B of **AI-Powered Libraries: A Practical Guide to Transforming Services and Operations** serves as a critical tool for evaluating a library's preparedness for AI adoption. This structured checklist enables library professionals to assess their institution's current infrastructure, staff capabilities, stakeholder engagement, and strategic alignment. By identifying strengths and areas for improvement, libraries can develop a tailored roadmap for successful AI implementation.

Purpose of the Readiness Assessment Worksheet

The worksheet is designed to:

1. **Evaluate Current Capabilities**: Understand existing resources, technology, and expertise.

2. **Identify Gaps**: Highlight areas that need enhancement before AI adoption.

3. **Align Goals**: Ensure AI initiatives support the library's mission and strategic objectives.

4. **Mitigate Risks**: Address potential challenges proactively to ensure smooth implementation.

Key Components of the Readiness Assessment Worksheet

1. Infrastructure Readiness

- **Questions to Assess**:

  o Does the library have a reliable IT infrastructure to support AI tools?

  o Are existing systems compatible with AI platforms?

o Is there sufficient storage and bandwidth for data-intensive applications?

- **Action Steps for Improvement:**

o Upgrade network capabilities and cloud storage as needed.

o Integrate scalable systems to accommodate future AI expansion.

2. Staff Expertise and Training

- **Questions to Assess:**

o Do staff have basic knowledge of AI concepts and tools?

o Is there a training plan to build AI-related skills?

o Are key staff members ready to lead AI projects?

- **Action Steps for Improvement:**

o Provide workshops on AI fundamentals and specific tools.

o Partner with vendors or local institutions for specialized training programs.

3. Stakeholder Engagement

- **Questions to Assess:**

o Are stakeholders (staff, patrons, and funders) aware of the benefits and implications of AI?

o Have stakeholders been involved in discussions about AI implementation?

o Is there a communication plan to address concerns or resistance?

- **Action Steps for Improvement:**

o Organize informational sessions to educate stakeholders about AI's potential.

o Develop a feedback mechanism to include stakeholder input in decision-making.

4. Financial and Resource Planning

- **Questions to Assess**:

o Is there a budget allocated for AI tools, implementation, and maintenance?

o Are funding sources identified, such as grants or partnerships?

o Does the library have a contingency plan for unforeseen costs?

- **Action Steps for Improvement**:

o Apply for technology grants or explore cost-sharing partnerships.

o Conduct a cost-benefit analysis to prioritize investments.

5. Strategic Alignment

- **Questions to Assess**:

o Do AI projects align with the library's mission and long-term goals?

o Are there clear objectives and success metrics for AI initiatives?

o Does the library have a phased implementation plan?

- **Action Steps for Improvement**:

o Define specific goals for AI adoption, such as improving user engagement or automating cataloging.

o Establish key performance indicators (KPIs) to measure success.

6. Risk Management

- **Questions to Assess**:

o   Are potential risks, such as data privacy concerns or technical failures, identified?

o   Is there a plan to address resistance from staff or patrons?

o   Are security protocols in place to protect user data?

- **Action Steps for Improvement:**

o   Develop data privacy and security policies aligned with legal standards.

o   Create a risk mitigation strategy, including staff training and pilot testing.

3. Using the Worksheet Effectively

Step 1: Conduct Self-Assessment

- Involve key stakeholders, including IT staff, library leadership, and front-line employees, in completing the worksheet.

- Use a rating scale (e.g., "Fully Prepared," "Partially Prepared," "Not Prepared") to evaluate each area.

Step 2: Prioritize Actions

- Focus on areas marked as "Not Prepared" or "Partially Prepared."

- Develop a timeline and allocate resources to address gaps.

Step 3: Update Regularly

- Reassess readiness at key project milestones to ensure continuous alignment with goals.

- Adjust strategies based on new insights or changes in technology.

Benefits of the Readiness Assessment Worksheet

1. **Structured Approach:**

o   Provides a clear framework for evaluating and preparing for AI adoption.

2. **Risk Reduction:**

o   Identifies potential challenges early, allowing for proactive solutions.

3. **Informed Decision-Making:**

o   Ensures decisions are based on a comprehensive understanding of the library's capabilities and needs.

4. **Stakeholder Buy-In:**

o   Engages staff and patrons in the planning process, fostering collaboration and support.

Conclusion

The Readiness Assessment Worksheet in Appendix B is an invaluable tool for libraries embarking on the journey of AI integration. By systematically evaluating infrastructure, staff expertise, financial planning, and stakeholder engagement, libraries can develop a robust foundation for successful AI implementation. This proactive approach minimizes risks, aligns efforts with strategic goals, and ensures that AI adoption delivers meaningful benefits for the library and its community.

Pilot Project Planning Template

The **Pilot Project Planning Template** in Appendix B of **AI-Powered Libraries: A Practical Guide to Transforming Services and Operations** is a practical tool designed to help libraries structure, execute, and evaluate AI pilot projects effectively. This template provides a comprehensive framework to define objectives, allocate resources, manage risks, and measure outcomes. By using this template, libraries can test AI solutions on a smaller scale, refine their approach based on real-world feedback, and ensure readiness for broader implementation.

Purpose of the Pilot Project Planning Template

1. **Test Feasibility**: Evaluate the practicality and effectiveness of AI solutions in a controlled environment.

2. **Identify Challenges**: Detect technical, operational, and user-related obstacles before full-scale deployment.

3. **Gather Data**: Collect performance metrics and user feedback to inform decision-making.

4. **Build Confidence**: Demonstrate the value of AI tools to stakeholders through measurable results.

Key Components of the Pilot Project Planning Template

1. Defining Objectives

- **Questions to Address**:

  o What specific problem or opportunity does the pilot project aim to address?

  o How will success be measured?

- **Examples**:

  o Objective: Test an AI chatbot's ability to handle 70% of routine patron inquiries within two weeks.

  o Success Metric: Reduction in average response time for patron queries by 50%.

2. Scope of the Pilot

- **Questions to Address**:

  o Which services or departments will be included in the pilot?

o   What is the duration of the pilot?

- **Examples**:

o   Scope: Implement an AI-powered catalog search in the digital resource department for three months.

o   Exclusion: Pilot excludes print resources to focus solely on digital content.

3. Resource Allocation

- **Questions to Address**:

o   What resources (staff, budget, equipment) are required for the pilot?

o   Who will manage and oversee the project?

- **Examples**:

o   Budget: Allocate $10,000 for software licensing and staff training.

o   Team: Assign a project manager and two technical support staff for implementation and monitoring.

4. Risk Management

- **Questions to Address**:

o   What are the potential risks associated with the pilot?

o   How will these risks be mitigated?

- **Examples**:

o   Risk: User resistance to the new AI tool.

o   Mitigation Strategy: Provide training sessions and informational materials for patrons and staff.

5. Stakeholder Engagement

- **Questions to Address**:

o Who are the key stakeholders, and how will they be involved?

o How will communication be maintained throughout the pilot?

- **Examples**:

o Stakeholders: Library staff, patrons, and local community groups.

o Communication Plan: Weekly progress updates via email and monthly review meetings.

6. Data Collection and Analysis

- **Questions to Address**:

o What data will be collected to evaluate the pilot's performance?

o How will the data be analyzed?

- **Examples**:

o Data Points: Number of chatbot interactions, user satisfaction ratings, and query resolution rates.

o Analysis: Compare pilot data with baseline metrics to assess improvements.

7. Timeline and Milestones

- **Questions to Address**:

o What are the major phases of the pilot, and what are their timelines?

o What deliverables are expected at each milestone?

- **Examples**:

o Timeline:

▪ Month 1: System setup and staff training.

- Month 2: Pilot launch and initial user feedback collection.

- Month 3: Data analysis and final report.

- **Milestones**:

o Completion of staff training.

o First 1,000 chatbot interactions logged.

o Submission of pilot evaluation report.

8. Post-Pilot Evaluation

- **Questions to Address**:

o How will the pilot's success or failure be determined?

o What are the next steps based on the evaluation?

- **Examples**:

o Evaluation: Compare pilot metrics against predefined success criteria.

o Next Steps: Scale successful projects to additional services or adjust based on lessons learned.

Using the Template Effectively

Step 1: Collaborate with Stakeholders

Involve staff, patrons, and other stakeholders in defining objectives and planning the pilot to ensure alignment with needs and expectations.

Step 2: Document Plans Thoroughly

Use the template to record all aspects of the pilot, including goals, resources, risks, and timelines.

Step 3: Monitor Progress

Regularly review progress against milestones and address any issues promptly.

Step 4: Adjust as Needed

Be flexible in adapting the pilot based on real-time feedback and observations.

Benefits of the Pilot Project Planning Template

1. **Reduces Risks**:

Identifies and resolves potential issues in a controlled setting.

2. **Enhances Decision-Making**:

Provides evidence-based insights to guide broader implementation.

3. **Builds Stakeholder Confidence**:

Demonstrates the feasibility and value of AI tools to staff, patrons, and funders.

4. **Optimizes Resources**:

Ensures efficient use of time, budget, and staff effort.

Conclusion

The Pilot Project Planning Template in Appendix B empowers libraries to test AI technologies systematically and strategically. By providing a clear roadmap for defining objectives, allocating resources, managing risks, and evaluating outcomes, this template ensures that pilot projects are well-structured and impactful. Through this approach, libraries can confidently adopt AI solutions, maximizing their benefits while minimizing disruptions.